Elizabeth Morton wearing her Order of Canada badge

The Morton Years

The Canadian Library Association 1946-1971

Researched and written by
Elizabeth Hulse
for the Ex Libris Association

With a Foreword by
W. Kaye Lamb

Toronto 1995

ISBN 0-9699645-0-1

Canadian Cataloguing in Publication Data

Hulse, Elizabeth, 1939-
The Morton Years: the Canadian Library Association, 1946-1971

Includes bibliographical references and index.
ISBN 0-9699645-0-1

1. Canadian Library Association – History.
2. Morton, Elizabeth Homer, 1903-1977.
I. Ex Libris Association. II. Title.

Z673.C35H8 1995 020'.6'2271 C95-932601-4

Illustrations courtesy of the Canadian Library Association unless otherwise indicated.

This book is dedicated to Canada's
library pioneers

Contents

Foreword

The title of this study is a richly deserved tribute to Elizabeth Morton, executive secretary of the Canadian Library Association for its first twenty-two years. The astonishing developments that took place between May 1944, when she arrived in Ottawa, and June 1946, when the founding conference of the Canadian Library Association met in Hamilton, would not, I am convinced, have taken place without her.

By a fortunate coincidence, Margaret (Madge) Gill, librarian of the National Research Council, had provided an office for the homeless Canadian Library Council, and she and Elizabeth had ambitions in common that made them a formidable team. Specifically, they were determined to see Canadian librarians united in a national association, and Canada provided with a National Library. A few able allies – notably Freda Waldon and Elizabeth Dafoe – gave strong support, but in the critical early days the group was small and feminine. Until it was apparent that the CLA would grow in stature and influence, senior male librarians tended to give their first allegiance to the old-established American Library Association.

They realized their ambitions over an eventful six-year period. Creation of the CLA came after two years of strenuous effort; another two saw the government committed in principle to a National Library, and two years later, in 1950, the Canadian Bibliographic Centre, the nucleus from which the National Library would grow, came into existence.

My appointment as dominion archivist brought me to Ottawa at the end of 1948. I was then past president of the CLA, and I was in close touch with Elizabeth for the next twenty years. I quickly learned to admire her vision, patience, and determination. Difficulties were to be tackled, not backed away from; if ever she was discouraged or downhearted, she concealed it well.

One light-hearted memory comes to mind. Both Elizabeth and her sister Mary suffered acutely from hay fever, but this was not widely known. Gifts of flowers would arrive, to their consternation. Our homes were not far apart, and every now and then we would see Elizabeth and Mary hurrying up the path to our front door, one arm holding the offending flowers at arm's length, the other holding a handkerchief to their noses. It was a typical Morton solution: it warded off the hay fever but assured the survival of many lovely flowers.

It would be difficult today to imagine Canada without the Canadian Library Association. It made librarians conscious of the fact that they were members of a nationwide profession and provided them with an annual forum and an opportunity to exchange information and experience, voice their opinions, and unite for common causes. It strengthened the east-west axis of the country at a time when many influences were tugging it from the south.

W. KAYE LAMB
FIRST NATIONAL LIBRARIAN

Preface

The first meeting of a small group of librarians was held in the fall of 1985 to discuss an idea. How could retired librarians keep in touch with each other? How could their recollections as part of the history of their profession be acquired and preserved? During 1986 a number of meetings were held in London, and on 6 November 1986 forty-one retired librarians met in Toronto through the courtesy of the Ontario Library Association and formed the Ex Libris Association.

At the second annual meeting, held on 19 November 1987, on the suggestion of Edith Jarvi, the association resolved "that the Council of the Canadian Library Association be petitioned to establish a trust account to receive donations to honour the memory of Elizabeth Morton, a driving force in the establishment of the Canadian Library Association and its first Executive Director," and further, "that the memorial to Elizabeth Morton take the form of a well researched and written, readable history of the Canadian Library Association including the early association of Canadians with the American Library Association and the many attempts to separate from that Association in the pursuit of a separate Canadian identity."

In 1988 the CLA established the fund, and the Board of the Ex Libris Association set a goal of $15,000 as it initiated its first campaign. The fund was supported by a very generous donation from Edith Jarvi on its establishment, and CLA's *Feliciter* in November 1988 published a fine article in support. In the spring of 1992 the target had been reached, and Janette White, president of Ex Libris, invited proposals from interested researchers/authors.

Members of the Ex Libris Association can be proud of their accomplishments in providing the initiative and in raising the funds, which came mostly from themselves. Members of the Board over several years are to be congratulated as they pursued this major project to such a successful conclusion. The library community should be grateful to the Ex Libris Association and the Canadian Library Association, with special thanks to Edith Jarvi for her initiative and financial support.

E. Stanley Beacock
Founder and Honorary President
Ex Libris Association

Acknowledgements

I am grateful to the Ex Libris Association for inviting me to write this history of the Canadian Library Association in its first quarter century. Members of the Elizabeth Homer Morton Project Committee read a draft of the manuscript and made many useful comments and suggestions. Some twenty long-time librarians recorded their reminiscences for the project. Their names are given in the bibliography, and many are quoted in the text. They contributed colour and humour to the narrative and a personal perspective that was frequently missing from the formal record. Without their memories, it would have been much more difficult to present a full portrait of the remarkable woman who directed the CLA for most of its first twenty-five years.

In Ottawa the staff of the Library Development Office at the National Library of Canada answered questions and located valuable material, which they allowed me to photocopy free of charge. Reference staff at the National Library and the National Archives of Canada were uniformly courteous and helpful. Karen Adams, the current executive director of the Canadian Library Association, gave me her perspective on the position. Her staff made files available to me and assisted with photocopying. I am particularly grateful to Myra Clowes, the volunteer archivist at the CLA office, for taking the time to locate photographs of the association's activities.

Diane Henderson, chief librarian of the Faculty of Information Studies at the University of Toronto, provided much valuable help. Without the rich resources of her library, many questions would have remained unanswered. Eric L. Swanick of the Legislative Library of New Brunswick supplied information about Elizabeth Morton's work with the New Brunswick Public Library Commission. John Marshall commented on his experiences with the Victoria

Public Library Board in 1954, and Bruce Peel helped to locate the source of an obscure quotation. To all those who assisted with this history, named and unnamed, I offer my thanks.

EH

1

"Glory Be! The Canadian Library Association"

The "two hundred and eight-five Canadians from every province of the Dominion and every type of library interest"[1] who descended on McMaster University in June 1946 had a single goal: the launching of a national organization devoted to the cause of libraries and librarianship. Freda F. Waldon of the Hamilton Public Library later commented, "Probably no new organization in Canada has ever been greeted with more joy and anticipation."[2] Armed with a draft constitution and a wide-ranging program, librarians talked, argued, and deliberated during the weekend of 14-16 June. "Free speech was the order of the day and the delegates discussed and amended until agreement was reached on activities, constitution, and finance."[3] It was an occasion long remembered as "marked by a sense of good comradeship and oneness of purpose. Discussion was everywhere – both indoors and out."[4] "One remembers particularly the happy feeling emanating from little groups of librarians chatting in the sun."[5] And from it all, the Canadian Library Association – Association Canadienne des Bibliothèques was born.

A "Pisgah-Glimpse of the Promised Land"

This was not the first attempt to form a national library organization. In fact, the CLA of 1946 had a lengthy prehistory. Canadian librarians had long been active in the American Library Association, which had been founded in 1876. On several occasions the ALA had met in Canada – in Montreal in 1900 and 1934, Ottawa in 1912, and Toronto in 1927 – and George H. Locke of the Toronto Public Library had served as president of the American organization in 1926-27. The close ties formed over the years were to prove both advantageous and problematic in the formation of a Canadian association. During the ALA conference in Montreal in June 1900, nine Canadians, including Charles Henry Gould of McGill University, James Bain, chief librarian of the Toronto Public Library, Edward Austin Hardy of Lindsay, R.J. Blackwell of the London Public Library, and E.A. Geiger of Brockville, met informally in Gould's office to discuss how cooperation might be achieved among Canadian libraries. At the end of the meeting, a motion was moved and carried that "we do now form the Canadian Library Association,"[6] and an organizing committee chaired by Bain was established. The committee met in Toronto in October that year. After "a good deal of discussion," it was decided that a nation-wide organization was impractical "at present," and instead a draft constitution was prepared for a provincial organization.[7] The Ontario Library Association came into existence at Easter 1901. Despite its name, it had no provincial limitations, and as the first and largest of the provincial organizations, it would frequently provide leadership on national issues in the future.

A second attempt to form a national association was made a quarter century later, again at an ALA conference, this time in Seattle in 1925. W.O. (William Oliver) Carson, inspector of libraries for the Ontario Department of Education, chaired three meetings on Canadian issues attended by the Canadians present at the conference, and a further meeting was arranged for Vancouver after ALA ended. Although there was general agreement on the need for a national organization, the best option was thought to be a "council made up of the librarians of the principal libraries of each province ... Among the subjects in which Canadian co-operation was thought desirable were Canadian bibliography, book-selection, professional training, the library and adult education and public documents."[8] Two years later, when ALA met in Toronto, about 190 Canadian librarians representing eight provinces met under the chairmanship of Fred Landon of the University of Western Ontario, president of the Ontario Library Association. They determined to form an organization whose membership would be "open not only to those engaged in professional library work, but also to those interested in the extension of the library movement in Canada."[9] The American Library Association was "pleased to extend the right hand of fellowship to the new Canadian Library Association which came to corporate life at the Toronto Conference."[10]

At the outset, it was felt that a comprehensive survey of library conditions across the country was needed. With the assistance of Carl H. Milam, executive secretary of ALA, a grant of $10,000 was obtained through the American organization from the Carnegie Corporation of New York for a "commission of enquiry." Throughout the summer of 1930, the commissioners – John Ridington of the University of British Columbia, Mary J.L. Black of the Fort William Public Library, and George H. Locke of the Toronto Public Library – travelled across the country visiting libraries of all types and sizes in every province and interviewing government officials, educators, labour leaders, newspaper editors, and businessmen. Their report, *Libraries in Canada: A Study of Library Conditions and Needs*, published three years later by the Ryerson Press in Toronto and the ALA, has been described as "one of the most significant and comprehensive documents in Canadian library history."[11] To the consternation of many, however, the commission argued against the establishment of a national library association:

This Commission has strong convictions as to the value of such an Association, with a small but thoroughly competent, technical staff, co-operating with other educational workers and agencies throughout the Dominion. For it can clearly be seen splendid avenues of usefulness. This Commission firmly believes that such an Association, properly organized and staffed, would do much to speed up library progress, and give to library workers incentive and enthusiasm. The scope of its proposed activities has been discussed, planned and accepted by those interested, from Atlantic to Pacific.

But this Commission reluctantly and regretfully reports that the organization of such an Association is out of the question, at least for the present.[12]

Nevertheless, when the American Library Association met again in Montreal in 1934, a body, to be made up of Black, Locke, Ridington, and eight others and to be called the Canadian Library Council, was formed. Its officers were announced a few days later. Carl Milam, who discussed the potential relationship of the council to ALA with those present, remarked, "I think it is inevitable that sometime in the future there will be an independent Canadian library association. I do not think that it can be avoided."[13] But nothing more was heard of this group, and it represented yet another failed attempt to organize. Several years would pass before a council of the same name came into life.

At the beginning of the Second World War, the Auxiliary War Services Branch of the Department of National Defence called a meeting to discuss library services to the armed forces, and it was when librarians found themselves unrepresented because the invitation had gone out to "national organizations" that they were spurred to unite. Informal discussion sprang up wherever librarians met. Margaret (Madge) S. Gill, chief librarian at the National Research Council and president of the Library Association of Ottawa for 1940-41, persuaded her organization to take the lead. On 20 November 1940 she and the corresponding secretary, Elizabeth Barr, send a letter to library associations and individuals inviting "an expression of opinion on the proposal that a national association be formed during the coming year." "The Library Association of Ottawa has become increasingly aware of the need in Canada for an association, national in its membership and scope, to deal with questions of vital concern to libraries and librarians, which, because of their national aspects, cannot be settled by regional associations. We believe that conditions due to the war have increased the need for prompt action if librarians are to meet the responsibilities that should reasonably be theirs."[14] The response was generally favourable, though some who replied cited lack of funds for travel, wartime conditions, and great distances as obstacles to such an organization.

Unknown to the Ottawa association, a committee of "Canadian library consultants," chaired by Charles R. Sanderson of the Toronto Public Library, had been established by ALA in October that year. It was announced in the December ALA *Bulletin*, just after the letter from Gill and Barr went out. Would the Ottawa initiative be considered anti-ALA? The question had preoccupied Canadian organizers before. The dilemma was resolved when members of the ALA committee and the Ottawa library association met over dinner on 27 January 1941, during a conference arranged by the educational services of the Canadian Legion. At the end of the evening, those present unanimously moved the establishment of a Canadian body to replace the committee: "That this meeting of librarians from every part of the Dominion feels that the proposals for the establishment of a Canadian Library Council offer the best prospect for the advancement of Canadian librarianship and for the development of a Canadian library organization."[15] The projects to be undertaken by the council included the submission of briefs or petitions to the federal government, the forwarding of a Canadian national library, the establishment of a library bulletin, the development of "friends of libraries" activities, a central bureau of information for and about libraries, field visitors for the extension of library activities in the country, and the publication of bibliographical material.

The Canadian Library Council met for the first time in October 1941 and officially came into existence in December 1943, when it was incorporated under the Companies Act. There were ten members, seven elected by the regional or provincial library associations and three appointed by the elected members. C.R. Sanderson served as the first chair. On the recommendation of the committee of Canadian consultants, ALA disbanded the committee and recognized the CLC as its advisory body on Canadian affairs. Through the good offices of the American association, the council obtained funding for the establishment of a central office, visits to libraries across the country, and the microfilming of newspapers of historic significance. Five annual payments totalling $20,000 were to be made by the Carnegie Corporation over the years 1944-48, and the Rockefeller Foundation provided $17,500 for microphotography and the services of a field visitor. With a modest budget of $4,000 in 1943-44, the council began the ambitious program set for it. Perhaps its greatest success, as Margaret Gill later wrote, would be "in recruiting Miss Elizabeth H. Morton" as executive secretary.[16]

"All of the Qualities We Want"

Elizabeth Homer Morton was born in Tunapuna, Trinidad, on 13 February 1903.[17] Her paternal grandfather, John Morton, a Presbyterian minister from Bridgewater, Nova Scotia, and his wife, Sarah Etter Silver, had gone to the Caribbean island in the 1860s to establish a mission to East Indian indentured labourers. Morton first visited the island a few years earlier on a ship employed in the West Indian trade, while he was recuperating from an illness, and he was appalled by the lack of provision for the labourers' spiritual welfare. With fellow Nova Scotian Kenneth Grant, he established schools, teachers training colleges, and other educational institutions. His work was carried on by his son – and Elizabeth's father – Harvey Holmes Morton. Her mother, Jessie Gordon Forbes, was from New Brunswick.

Elizabeth was the eldest of six children, three girls and three boys. Her father, educated at the universities of Edinburgh and Marburg, had also studied music in Berlin. Her mother was an enthusiastic singer and storyteller, but her eyesight was limited, and the children, as soon as they knew how, would take turns reading aloud to her. Both Elizabeth's father and her grandfather were avid book collectors. She and her brothers and sisters thus grew up in a household devoted to music and literature, passions she would retain all her life. Elizabeth's grandfather John Morton introduced her to book production when he taught her to collate a Hindi hymn-book he had printed on his own hand press. In a talk that she gave in 1964, she described the multicultural world she and her siblings had known: the calypso music, the Ashanti stories from Africa told by the cook and the nurse, the Portuguese, Dutch, and French history of the islands related by their grandparents, the Hindi hymns the family sang on Sundays, and their mother's retelling of the Scottish, English, and Irish folklore of her ancestors.[18] Every five years the family would spend the summer in Canada and return "speaking re-Canadianized English."[19] But according to someone who knew Elizabeth later, she retained the "sing-song accent of the Islands." When she travelled across Canada by train, West Indian porters "recognized her as one of their own and treated her to premier service."[20]

In 1919 Elizabeth Morton left Trinidad to complete her schooling at the Saint John High School in New Brunswick. She lived with her maternal grandfather, the judge James Gordon Forbes. Mr Justice Forbes, then in his eighties, had had a remarkable career and was a lively raconteur. In his youth he had campaigned for Confederation in the Maritime provinces. Morton would later say in reference to him, "I have been brought up with politics in my blood."[21] She attended Dalhousie University, where she obtained a BA with distinction in English and history in 1926. At Dalhousie she was a member of Archibald MacMechan's Inky Finger Club in English XI. For her, writing was an avocation never fully expressed, though she would put her love of language to good use in editing the publications of the Canadian Library Council and the Canadian Library Association.

Morton had intended to become a teacher, but a summer spent teaching in Oban on Cape Breton Island, a nearly bookless community, aroused her interest in library work. However, she completed the six-week training session at the Nova Scotia Normal School in Truro and obtained a type A certificate. After spending the summer of 1926 at the Toronto Public Library, she attended the Ontario Library School, held by the Department of Education in the main building of TPL from September to December. Hers was a remarkable class that included Angus Mowat, later inspector of public libraries for Ontario, and the future bibliographer Marie Tremaine, both to be lifelong friends. Early in 1927 Morton rejoined the staff of TPL, but after sixteen months spent in the cataloguing department, she returned to New Brunswick to care for her grandfather after the death of an aunt. She taught English and history to night students at the Saint John Vocational School and organized libraries at the school and the Simms brush factory. For an eight-month period in 1930-31 she served as secretary of the New Brunswick Public Library Commission, which had been set up in 1929 to coordinate and promote library services in the province. At the request of Premier J.B.M. Baxter, she surveyed the Legislative

Library. In the words of its recent historian, "Her clear and detailed report indicated that the Library was moribund with the exception of the fiction collection and recommended that the Library be reorganized to serve the Legislature rather than the public. Her advice was ignored."[22]

Together with their grandfather, Elizabeth and Mary Morton moved to Toronto in 1931, and Elizabeth was able to return to the Toronto Public Library, this time as a reference librarian. Katharine L. Ball would later recall a fine example of her flair for reference work. A patron had asked for a book called – he thought – *The Red Boat*, author unknown, and Morton produced just what he wanted: *The Rubaiyat of Omar Khayyam*! At TPL she was in charge of the private press collection and was able to indulge her love of fine books.[23] In 1936 she was appointed part-time secretary-treasurer of the Ontario Library Association, a position she held until 1943. At the OLA she first demonstrated her ability for administrative work. Marie Tremaine credited her with reforming the organization:

> During her period of office the Association changed from an organization supported mainly by institutional memberships to one in which most Ontario librarians felt they had an individual professional stake ... To the Secretary-Treasurer's personality, her realization of our professional needs, and her ready practical suggestions in policy-making go much of the credit for making the O.L.A. an Ontario *librarians* association. Miss Morton's term of office was also marked by increasing contacts and cooperation with other provincial library associations across Canada. There developed a growing realization of our common problems and of the potential importance of libraries in the cultural and social life of the Dominion. A realization, too, of our need to get together and pull together to bring libraries to public attention.[24]

Morton also served as Canadian representative on the subscription books committee of the American Library Association. Her work for the committee provided her with an "opportunity to study book production and sales methods, particularly as they affect the small and medium sized library, to survey current reference works and see how far they meet Canadian library needs. Her ... desk became a little information centre for librarians from Vancouver to Saint John."[25] In both these functions, as in her earlier work for the New Brunswick Public Library Commission, she was, unknowingly, preparing for her career with the Canadian Library Association. While at TPL, Morton took graduate courses in bibliography and historiography at the University of Toronto. She resigned from the OLA in 1943 to do postgraduate work in the United States, but her studies were postponed by staff shortages at the library. It would not be the only time her educational plans were put off indefinitely.

After the Canadian Library Council's first meeting in the fall of 1941, the members had exchanged letters about the difficulties of operating without office staff. Edgar S. Robinson of the Vancouver Public Library wrote to Sanderson in December, "I feel strongly that no organization setting out to do what we have planned can possibly survive on a completely voluntary basis ... I think it would be desirable to have a senior librarian who could act more or less as an executive secretary immediately under the direction of the chairman."[26] Yet how to hire a responsible person to travel across the country and run an office on the CLC's modest budget was a dilemma. Indeed, until it began to receive the annual grant from the Carnegie Corporation in February 1944, it had no budget at all. In January that year Margaret Gill, now chairing the council, told Sanderson, "Very shortly after our last meeting in Winnipeg I suddenly realized that the person who, in my mind, embodies most, if not all, of the qualities we want in the Executive Secretary of the C.L.C. is Miss Elizabeth Morton of the T.P.L. Reference Staff ... I do not know what salary would be necessary to tempt her or whether I am risking your everlasting ire by suggesting that another member of your staff be purloined! What do you think?"[27] Sanderson was pessimistic that "she would be tempted to change. With the recent 10% increase in salaries, hers would go to $2,200. I don't imagine the C.L.C. can afford more than this, or enough more to create a bait, besides which she has a good many years accumulated pension rights here. She was considered for the Jamaica job, having been born in the West Indies and her family still living there. But she wouldn't look at it as anything short of a permanent post."[28]

Nevertheless, Elizabeth Morton was tempted. The council could only offer her $2,000 a year, but would allow her to spend time each summer on research at Columbia University, a project that, as she said, would "keep the Secretary alive to the changes in the Library field."[29] (She would, in fact, go to the University of Chicago and combine her studies there with observation at the ALA head office.) Gill was able to report that Morton was "sufficiently interested in the job to be done to sacrifice the advantages offered by T.P.L."[30] After some skirmishes with the bureaucracy of the wartime National Selective Service and the Unemployment Insurance Commission, with whom her transfer had to be cleared, Elizabeth Homer Morton arrived to take up her new responsibilities in Ottawa in May 1944.

Three tasks awaited her: coordinating nearly a dozen provincial and special-interest briefs to the House of Commons Special Committee on Reconstruction and Re-establishment (chaired by James Gray Turgeon), editing the council's first bulletin, and assisting the *Wilson Library Bulletin* with a special Canadian number, to be published in November. Sanderson had told Morton, when he said goodbye to her in Toronto, that the brief "just won't jell for me."[31] But she had faced a similar dilemma in 1938 as secretary of the Ontario Library Association, when W. Stewart Wallace had thrown up his hands over a brief to the Royal Commission on Dominion-Provincial Relations saying, "Miss Morton, do they agree on anything?"[32] She set to work on all three tasks in the cramped quarters provided by the National Research Council library.

The first issue of the CLC *Bulletin* appeared in October 1944. Two thousand copies were mailed out by an "addressing bee" organized by librarians in the civil service. Margaret Gill was able to announce that the CLC brief, "Library Service for Canada," had been presented to the Turgeon committee in August. Appended to the brief were English and French editions of a pamphlet by Nora Bateson, *Rural Canada Needs Libraries*, and an article on "A National Library" by Elizabeth Dafoe from the May issue of the magazine *Food for Thought*. Several projects were in the planning stage, including a list of Canadian government documents and cooperation with the National Film Board on a film eventually produced as *Library on Wheels*. The CLC *Bulletin* was greeted with congratulations and subscriptions from as far away as Georgia. For librarians in Canada isolated from one another by great distances, it provided informative articles, news notes, and listings of available positions. From Kentville, Nova Scotia, came the comment, "You have made many of us living at a distance from reference libraries feel that there was a door, leading directly ... into your office."[33]

On 27 April 1945 the council sponsored a round table "to consider matters of interest to libraries from a national point of view"[34] – specifically the establishment of a national library – to which representatives of national organizations and government departments were invited. Using funds provided by the Rockefeller Foundation, Richard E. Crouch of the London Public Library, Elizabeth Morton, and others made a series of visits to libraries from Prince Edward Island to British Columbia. One of the aims of the Canadian Library Council, when it was formed in 1941, had been the "establishment of a permanent and self-supporting Canadian Library Organization."[35] During its meeting in April 1945, the council discussed the possibility of forming a division of ALA, but voted instead to take the preliminary steps to form a Canadian organization during the coming year. In October it reported that those provincial associations which had held their annual conferences were "unanimous in directing the Canadian Library Council to proceed with the organization of a Canadian Library Association and with the proposed survey of Canadian library resources."[36] An organizational conference was announced for the summer of 1946 just before the ALA conference. A tentative constitution and bylaws, incorporating changes suggested by the provincial associations, appeared in the *Bulletin* in June 1946. The results of the survey, as they related to public libraries, were presented as an interim report. Its title, *Libraries in the Life of the Canadian Nation*, provided the theme of the organizational conference.

"Make No Small Plans": Hamilton, 1946

The Hamilton conference of 1946 was to set the model for the future both in the form it took and in the issues it addressed. Following a panel discussion on Friday morning, 14 June, and an address by Charles F. Burke, dean of arts and science at McMaster University and chairman of the Hamilton Public Library Board, Gerhard R. Lomer of McGill University spoke about "The Background of the Canadian Library Association." He reminded the delegates of previous attempts to form an association, "when there was hopeful talk of the future and an occasional Pisgah-glimpse of the promised land of librarianship."[37] He urged the delegates to see that "this convention does not fail in the purpose for which it was called ... Let this day be the V-Day of our profession in Canada in its war against apathy, ignorance, narrow-mindedness, selfishness, and regionalism of any kind."[38] A panel discussion that followed focused on standards of training and salaries and on library legislation, particularly as it related to certification, the role of government commissions and services, and tax support.

The first afternoon was devoted to the constitution, and according to one delegate, the discussion "developed into a general wrestling match in which nearly everybody had something to say."[39] C.R. Sanderson chaired the evening session, which was addressed by C. Cecil Lingard on "The Implications of UNESCO for Canada" and then heard briefly from the Hon. Paul Martin, secretary of state in the federal government. On Saturday morning there was further discussion of the constitution. The nominating committee then presented the first slate for the new association:

President: Freda F. Waldon, Hamilton Public Library
First vice-president and president-elect: W. Kaye Lamb, University of British Columbia

Second vice-president: Joseph-Antoine Brunet, Montreal Catholic School Commission
Treasurer: Hugh Gourlay, Edmonton Public Library

Elizabeth Morton would continue as executive secretary. The afternoon was devoted to workshops, and in the evening, the conference was addressed by Luther H. Evans, librarian of Congress, on "The National Library in the Life of the Nation." After a public relations clinic conducted by J.-A. Brunet, the new president gave a brief speech.

In the discussion of the constitution, a number of francophone delegates proposed that in addition to its English name, the organization be called the Association Canadienne des Bibliothèques "so as to make it evident to everybody that Canada is a bilingual country."[40] A significant change had been made to the make-up of the governing council as proposed in the first draft of the constitution, which had called for a body composed, like the Canadian Library Council, of representatives elected by the provincial library associations and of members at large chosen by those representatives. Instead, in response to "the request of various members who felt a more democratic procedure should be followed,"[41] councillors were to be elected by the membership at large.

Resolutions passed at the conference concerned such issues as support for UNESCO, a national library for Canada, rural library service, and salary standards. In presenting the report of the activities committee, Waldon warned that the association must not attempt too much "until we have a headquarters staff equipped to handle more activities."[42] Nevertheless, a broad program was approved. The new organization was first to carry on the activities of the Canadian Library Council:

- a headquarters office which would serve as a clearing-house for library information;
- Canadian library publications;
- a scheme of library visits;
- liaison with (a) the federal government on national matters, such as the distribution of government documents, postal rates, and custom duties, (b) all organizations concerned with education, information, recreation, and cultural activities, and (c) ALA and other national associations;
- public relations concerning libraries at the national level; and
- conferences of library interests at a national level.

As the CLA grew in membership and experience, it should strive to develop:

- library standards for Canada; including (a) standards of service for communities, (b) standards of librarianship, and (c) standard library legislation to assist any body planning such legislation;
- library placement;
- library exchanges within Canada and abroad of staff, materials, etc.;
- interlibrary loans of professional library information;
- a list of library surveyors with expert knowledge to give advice;
- encouragement for the compiling of Canadian reference books; and
- support for efforts to promote library training.

The conference concluded with "a feeling of solidarity and accomplishment in achieving something for the library movement in Canada."[43] The delegates went away full of enthusiasm for the new cause. Bruce B. Peel, then a young librarian at the University of Saskatchewan, recalls that colleagues returned from "the Hamilton 'Woodstock' ... with the missionary zeal of born again Christians. In our library Ruth Murray was the zealot. On pay day we crossed the street to a bank to cash our cheques. First pay day Ruth stood athwart my path and demanded that I take a CLA membership which was $10 or $15. I pleaded that having been a student the previous year, I was impoverished. Ruth said she would let me off, but would be back blocking my path" on the next pay day.[44] He had no option but to join.

2

CLA at Work: Projects and Activities, 1946-55

The Canadian Library Association – Association Canadienne des Bibliothèques (CLA – ACB) began operations in the space that had been provided for the Canadian Library Council by the National Research Council. Until the CLC could be wound up, this office would be maintained and Elizabeth Morton would spend some time here each week. But in September 1946 she was able to report that "a very pleasant and roomy office" had been found for CLA at 74 Stanley Avenue, a ten-minute walk from the NRC.[1] Purchased for this office were "a new typewriter, 2 typing desks, 3 chairs, a second-hand table, a book-case and $2.00 worth of orange crates for shelving."[2] A second, portable typewriter was borrowed from a member. The staff initially consisted of a part-time clerical assistant and a part-time librarian, in addition to the executive secretary. In February, two full-time clerical assistants were acquired. When winter arrived, the office proved less pleasant. The furnace "was condemned by the City Fire Department and hardship reigned during the five weeks that an oil furnace was being installed. The office was rescued from suffering by Mr. and Mrs. F.C. Jennings, the good neighbours of 70 Stanley Avenue, and was accommodated in their recreation room. Their kindness will never be forgotten or the hot coffee Mrs. Jennings so thoughtfully supplied!"[3]

In any case, by March the following year, the building had been sold, and Morton and her small staff were forced to move. Office space was extremely scarce in Ottawa after the war. When a suitable office was found at 46 Elgin Street, in a building known as Central Chambers, there was no time to consult with the executive. Morton and Margaret Gill decided to accept the premises, and the staff moved in on 3 April. The new location was just a block away from Parliament Hill, the Chateau Laurier, and the railway station. The space was divided into a general office, a small office for Morton, and a stockroom for publications. She sent Freda Waldon a sketch of the new premises just before the move and was able to report that "staff is working together nicely so I see promise of catching up on the back work, cold is better, and migraine lessening."[4] Elizabeth Morton and her sister Mary, now librarian at the National Health and Welfare library, were "still homeless but we can store our things and it isn't so important about us as to get the office located."[5] By this time, the office had acquired a mascot. "Her name is Veronica and she is pale grey, felix domesticus. She has presented the office with two offspring who have been named William and Mary."[6] An operational budget for the nine months beginning 1 September 1946 totalled $5,082.13, of which $3,177.30 went for salaries and the rest for rent, office services, stationery, postage, and equipment.[7]

An immediate concern for the executive and secretary was incorporation of the new organization. Until it was incorporated, the CLC could not be wound up and the money from the Carnegie Corporation and the Rockefeller Foundation turned over to CLA. Incorporation by act of Parliament would have been preferable since it would have allowed greater flexibility in the constitution, but would have been prohibitively expensive. Instead the CLA – ACB was incorporated by letters patent under the Companies Act, a process that entailed lengthy manoeuvring with the secretary of state's department. A number of changes had to be made to the constitution. Letters patent were finally issued to the organization on 26 November 1947. The CLC subsequently surrendered its charter, and its assets were turned over to the CLA. As a corporation, CLA was required to hold an annual general meeting regardless of what arrangements might be made for a conference. Changes to the constitution also had to follow the regulations for corporations and be approved by the secretary of state's department.

The association was to be administered by an executive board (board of directors) made up of a president, a first vice-president and president-elect, a second vice-president, and a treasurer, all elected annually by the membership, together with the executive secretary and the past president. Among its duties, the executive board reviewed all membership applications, examined the annual estimates and approved the budget, appointed the executive secretary, and set salaries for employees. Only "library members" – that is, persons "who are or have been employed as librarians or who have graduated from a library school" – were eligible for election to the executive board. The Council – made up of nine councillors elected by the membership at large, the members of the executive board, and section chairs – was the legislative body of the association. It determined all policies; reviewed the action of officers, committees, and the executive board; considered matters of professional and public interest referred to it by committees or the board; appointed standing committees; and reported annually to the membership.

According to the constitution, "Special interest sections may be constituted as provided for in the By-laws." Sections were required to appoint a chair and present a financial statement at the annual meeting. They were "autonomous, in regard to elections and appointments, choosing their own officers and setting-up their committees as needed."[8] Section fees could be levied; the sections could also petition the Council for financial aid. At the 1947 conference, the committee responsible for the constitution had proposed an amendment specifying that sections could be established "on petition of twenty members in good standing."[9] In the event, the article on sections proved problematic in the incorporation process, and this specification was omitted from the constitution in its final 1947 form. After the founding convention, six interest groups had requested that they be allowed to explore sectional status. Two sections were formed in time for the 1947 conference: a cataloguing section and the Canadian Association of Children's Librarians (which in fact predated the CLA). At that conference the trustees passed a resolution to form a section. The reference section was established in 1948 and the young people's section in 1950. That devoted to college and university libraries was formally constituted as the research libraries section in 1949. (The names of sections would be changed over the years, special interests would regroup, and some sections would become constituent associations.)

The constitution also provided for the appointment of committees. They would quickly provide the principal mechanism by which much of the work of the association was carried out. In 1950 President Kathleen R. Jenkins commented that an association "such as ours, obviously needs many committees. Perhaps not quite so obvious is the perpetual need for review of these committees, in order that their number may be kept within reasonable bounds, that inactive ones may be abolished and that new ones may be formed to meet new situations."[10] This was the function of the committee on committees, a subcommittee of the board established in 1948. It reviewed applications for new sections and committees, drew up their terms of reference, recommended the cancellation or suspension of committees no longer deemed necessary, appointed committee chairs and received their nominations for members, and reviewed applications for financial aid. In the first ten years of the association's existence, some thirty-two committees were formed. Some, such as those on budget and finance, election, membership, nominating, and resolutions, were essential to the functioning of the organization and constituted standing committees. A number provided liaison with other bodies, such as the ALA, other library associations, the Canadian Association for Adult Education, the Canadian Radio Council, and book publishers. Some were directed at specific projects and would be disbanded as soon as their work – a brief to a royal commission, for example – was completed, and others were special-interest groups that eventually evolved into sections.

Microfilming Historic Newspapers

The microfilming of historic Canadian newspapers had been a project of the Canadian Library Council, and a major part of the grant received in 1942 from the Rockefeller Foundation had been directed to this undertaking. Indeed, the project seems to have been first formally proposed by Charles F. McCombs of the New York Public Library, who made a tour of Canadian libraries for the foundation in 1941. In a letter to the foundation in December that year, he called it "Mr. Sanderson's project."[11] Historians had also been aware of the value of microfilming, and the *Canadian Historical Review* had editorialized on the subject on several occasions. The Rockefeller grant of $15,000 was to be spent over three years beginning in May 1942. However, because of the war, a camera could not be obtained, and the foundation was repeatedly asked to extend the deadline for the grant to be used. In fact, a camera did not arrive until February 1947, after the CLA had been established and the project turned over to the new organization. CLA faced a deadline of April 1948, at which point the grant would be withdrawn. The camera was initially set up at Microfilming Services in Toronto (later called Preston Microfilming Services), but filming done there proved unsatisfactory: newspapers were carelessly handled and the quality of the work was poor.[12] In September the camera was moved to Ottawa, where work could be better supervised. Space was provided in the basement of the Public Archives building.

The project was intended to be self-supporting after the initial grant. Films were first priced so that the cost of microfilming each title would be covered by the sale of five copies. Any sales over that number would provide capital to be put back into the project. Five copies proved too optimistic, and in 1949 the number was reduced to three; it would later be increased to four. At the Council meeting in June 1947, there was some discussion as to how the grant was to be apportioned, whether by region of the country, by population, or even by CLA membership. Of the initial grant, $5,000 was assigned to the camera (approximately $3,400), travel, and printing expenses, while $2,000 each was allotted to the Maritime provinces, Quebec, Ontario, Manitoba and Saskatchewan, and Alberta and British Columbia. A compromise had always to be maintained between what should be filmed and what would sell. In 1953 Robert H. Blackburn, then chair of the microfilm committee, reported that many papers of interest to historians and genealogists might never be filmed because of their limited local appeal, and the association did not have enough working capital to film any really long runs. It was not until later, when the project obtained additional funds from Canadian sources, that some newspapers of limited appeal were filmed. The principal costs were for the time needed to collate and photograph the papers and check the films and for freight charges for shipping the papers to Ottawa and returning them to the lending institution.

The project came under the direction of a committee initially chaired by Robert M. Hamilton, assistant librarian of Parliament. In 1949 he was replaced by Robert Blackburn of the University of Toronto Library. Willard E. Ireland served briefly in 1953-54. He was followed by James J. Talman of the University of Western Ontario, who headed the committee from 1954 to 1971. The first committee under Hamilton worked very hard to meet the April 1948 deadline. Elsie McLeod Murray (later Jury) collated files of newspapers and prepared directions for the camera operators, and Martha Shepard of the Toronto Public Library checked the positive film for errors in photographing. Other members of the association assisted with the collating of newspapers in their respective provinces. Eventually, some filming would be done by provincial archives, and the project in turn supplemented its income with contract work for various Canadian and American institutions.

The first catalogue appeared in 1948. Now a rare item, it was "a handsome pamphlet with a bright red cover and included an illustration and newspaper file for each province, except, of course, Newfoundland."[13] The high quality of the catalogue was possible because some money remained from the grant, and it "created a good public image."[14] As the introduction explained, the committee had chosen for filming

> those journals which gave leadership in political thought, reflected the opinions of the

various sections of the country, and recorded its settlement, commercial enterprises, railway development, etc. ... When the Association's Committee had to make a choice between two papers of equal importance, the choice was influenced by whether or not the files were scattered. The paper with the scattered file was chosen. One title required files from seven depositories in Canada and the United States and the film still shows issues missing.[15]

During the 1948 conference, which was held in Ottawa, a delegation presented Prime Minister Mackenzie King with a handsome leather box containing a microfilm copy of the *Colonial Advocate*, published by his grandfather William Lyon Mackenzie.[16]

Subsequent catalogues appeared in the CLA *Bulletin* and separately in pamphlet form. They were issued in 1949, 1950, 1953, 1955, and 1957.[17] Each catalogue listed only the new titles, and by 1957 it was apparent that users would be required to work their way through an ever-increasing number of lists. In 1959 the committee, under the supervision of Sheila A. Egoff, put together a cumulative catalogue in loose-leaf form which could be continuously revised and updated; an index would be provided each year. The catalogue eventually extended to three binders.

The microfilm project struck a best seller in one of its first choices for Alberta. The *Calgary Eye-Opener* by 1968 would have sold twenty-nine copies, though the record among newspaper titles would be set by the *Globe*, with forty copies sold by that year. The average number of copies over the years would prove to be fourteen.[18] The possibility of CLA acting as a central repository for libraries unable to purchase films was discussed early in the project, but this was felt to be the function of a national library, and the association could not afford the space or staff time required. In any case, a system of loans could potentially reduce sales, and libraries that could not afford films were unlikely to be able to purchase a microfilm reader either.

The original terms of reference for the microfilm committee had called for "the duplication of Canadian newspapers, pamphlets, broadsides, periodicals, books, maps, etc., by the microfilm process."[19] The 1953 catalogue listed the mail-order catalogues of the T. Eaton Company, a rich source for social and economic history that had been suggested by the noted historian A.R.M. Lomer a few years earlier. The project also filmed the debates of the Legislative Council and Assembly of the Province of Canada and of the federal houses after Confederation for the period 1846-74, as they were reported in the newspapers and preserved in scrapbooks at the Library of Parliament. To promote the project a newsletter called *To Keep You Posted about the Microfilm Project* was launched in 1954. By the following year, approximately one hundred newspapers titles had been filmed and sales made to some ninety-two institutions in Canada, the United States, and abroad.

Joyce Sowby, who joined the CLA office in 1953 and became one of the secretaries of the project a few years later, describes how it functioned: "The Microfilm Committee decided on the titles to be filmed. Then, the Secretary borrowed the volumes from across the country; prepared them for filming by our camera operator, Roland Guttadauria, who did his filming after he had finished his milk route; sent the reels of film to be processed by Preston Microfilming Services in Toronto, who held the negatives after they had been checked by the Secretary and any necessary retakes taken. [At first the negatives had had to be sent to Rochester for processing.] The Secretary, with members of the Microfilm Committee, prepared historical notes on each title, which were published as 'Microfilm news notes,' and sent to interested libraries and institutions in Canada, the United States and Britain. The finished product was costed, orders were received, filled by Preston Microfilming Services and mailed from Ottawa."[20]

The Canadian Index

Among the bibliographical publications proposed when the Canadian Library Council was established in 1941 was an index to Canadian periodicals. Such an index had long been considered desirable, and several attempts had been made to produce one. When Canadian librarians gathered in Seattle in 1925, the "possibility of indexing selected Canadian periodicals was briefly discussed and a committee named."[21] The Windsor Public Library began publishing a *Canadian Periodical Index* in 1928, but the project was abandoned after four years. From 1938, staff in the circulation department of the University of Toronto Library had been compiling an index with the same title, which was still being published when CLA was founded in 1946, though it faced an uncertain future. By arrangement with the Public Libraries Branch of the Ontario Department of Education, the quarterly issues of the index appeared in the *Ontario Library Review*, and the Public Libraries Branch issued the annual cumulations. (CLA would publish a cumulation of the 1938-47 index in 1966 using the original index cards, which had been turned over to the association by the University of Toronto Library.) In an article in the CLA *Bulletin* in December 1947, Elizabeth

Morton noted that it was just a hundred years since the first periodical index. Yet the *Reader's Guide to Periodical Literature* currently indexed only three Canadian magazines (*Canadian Forum*, *Canadian Geographical Journal*, and *Queen's Quarterly*) out of some 129 titles, most American, while the *International Index* covered only four Canadian titles.

The activities committee of CLA, in its inaugural report of 1946, urged that an index of Canadian periodicals be given priority. Plans for the index were presented at the annual conference the following year, and the association was able to secure a three-year grant totalling $12,000 from the Carnegie Corporation to cover the start-up costs. It was hoped that the index would be self-supporting, though non-profit. "To make the *Index* available to the small library, the price can only be kept low if the subscription list is large, and then only by a system of service payments on an income basis."[22] Dorothy B. Chatwin (née Kelly), a graduate in French from the University of British Columbia and with a degree from the University of Washington Library School, was hired as part-time editor in the spring of 1947, and work began on the project. The first monthly number of the *Canadian Index: A Guide to Periodicals and Documentary Films* appeared the following January (documentary films were added after the first three issues). It provided access by author and subject to fifty-six titles, of which one-quarter were French-language publications. The first titles chosen for inclusion were in the areas of culture and the humanities, "general periodicals in greatest demand in the public, university and larger special libraries – magazines on current events, economics, public administration, cultural affairs, and university quarterlies, with special attention to the work of Canadian writers, artists, etc."[23] It was intended that coverage would eventually be extended to three other groups: science and technology, education, and agriculture. Subject headings were in English, with cross-references from French headings. The first annual cumulation appeared in 1949, and a twelve-year cumulation would eventually be issued in 1962.

The year after the Carnegie grant came to an end (1951-52), the *Index* faced a deficit of more than $3,000. Staff were cut, work methods simplified, and the number of titles indexed reduced from sixty-six to fifty-one. When the National Library was established, it provided assistance by assuming the printing costs of the annual cumulations. By 1955 the *Index* was able to report a "solvent financial position," but it still struggled to be "reasonably close to self-supporting."[24] Subscriptions had risen slowly from 262 in the first year to 337 in 1954. The publication now had an associate editor, Margaret Wodehouse, and an assistant editor, Ruth Mulholland, in addition to the editor, who also served as executive secretary in Morton's absence and as secretary for the project to evaluate library education. They worked out of a small room at 56 Sparks Street and were assisted by secretarial staff from the main office. Isabel Lee Bradley, who arrived at CLA in 1956 and would become the *Index*'s editor the following year, recalls how it was put together. "At this time the Index was very much a manual operation. Subject headings were written directly into the serials, cards typed, sorted, pasted up, edited, then reproduced into monthly editions and cumulated annually. The annual cumulation was edited and proofread in the Index office, but shipped out for commercial printing."[25]

Other Publications

The *Bulletin* was another of the projects of the Canadian Library Council to be carried on by the new association. When it had been begun in 1944, it had to be "attractive for an infinitesimal small sum."[26] The early issues were limited to half a dozen pages, and each issue was printed in a different colour ink on white paper. The fourth number introduced illustrations by artist Doris Meisel, who had worked for the Toronto Public Library before moving to Ottawa during the war. The CLA *Bulletin* continued the numbering of its predecessor and initially its format. Elizabeth Morton, who served as editor for CLA publications in addition to her other duties, was determined that all publications "should be a credit to the Association, and to Canada – exact as to scholarship, readable in style and attractive in format and typography."[27] With the issue for December 1946, the *Bulletin* had a new format. Amusing cartoons, provided by artists in the animation department of the National Film Board, were scattered through the pages "just like the *New Yorker.*" The following number saw the appointment of Dorothy Wright of the National Research Council as art editor. As she completed her term as president in 1947, Freda Waldon wrote to George Dunning of the NFB to express her appreciation for the contribution made by NFB artists.

> It really has been thrilling that we have been able to put out the most attractive library magazine on the continent in our first year of organization. While Miss Morton must be given the credit for the very good matter that has gone into the Bulletin, we could not have made the appearance so attractive without your help. The illustrations and the general layout have certainly lent distinction to our new venture ...

... It is something new in library circles hardly to be able to wait for the next number of a professional magazine to see what it will be like *this* time ...

... further evidence of the new life that is stirring in this country. We are part of an intellectual and artistic ferment that is creating a distinctive culture in Canada.[28]

In October 1946 it had been announced that the *Bulletin* would appear in October, December, February, April, and June. The subscription was set at $1.00 a year. With volume 4 it had been hoped the publication would become monthly, but by the end of the year the frequency was reduced to bimonthly. Initially printed in Ottawa, the *Bulletin* was moved to Toronto and then to the Charters Publishing Company in Brampton. In February 1947 it began to carry advertising, and Victor W. Dyas was appointed advertising agent. The publication became almost totally dependent on advertising for its survival. Just how important this revenue was is demonstrated by the budget for the year 1950-51. Of the $5,612.50 spent for typing, art cuts, and printing, subscriptions accounted for $836.72, membership fees prorated at 70.3 cents for $943.09, and advertising for the balance of $3,832.69.[29]

David W. Foley, in a article on the CLA as publisher, described the *Bulletin* as an institutional workhorse. In addition to articles on aspects of libraries and librarianship, news notes, and the association's announcements, it was frequently obliged to carry reports and conference proceedings, sometimes filling in for separate publications when funds were scarce. As the committee responsible for the *Bulletin* reported in 1951, though this practice assisted the work of the association, it "does not create for the *Bulletin* a reputation as a magazine carrying the most timely and provocative articles about books and libraries."[30] Brief book reviews were introduced in December 1946 but dropped shortly after, when they "did not appear early enough to aid libraries in book selection."[31] A new publication, *Feliciter*, would join the *Bulletin* in January 1956 to keep members up to date, and the *Bulletin* would eventually become *Canadian Library* and later the *Canadian Library Journal*.

The activities committee in 1946 had recommended a program of "Canadian library publications" and had identified some forty reference tools that were needed. As Waldon later stated, "We wanted Canadian cataloguing aids to supplement the service of the Library of Congress, a national union catalogue, better lists of dominion and provincial government documents, and a national bibliography of current literature."[32] The CLA Council soon found itself offered manuscripts on a variety of subjects not closely related to library work. "It was laid down as a matter of policy that the Association should restrict itself to the publishing of library tools."[33] For other reference works, the association's role would be to encourage their compilation, advise on content, assist in finding a publisher, and promote prepublication orders. A subject index to the proceedings and transactions of the Royal Society of Canada for the years 1907-37 was issued by CLA in 1947 as the first of a series of Reference Publications. Part of the cost was defrayed by the London Public Library and Art Museum. *Canadian Public Library Laws, 1946*, an unofficial consolidation of all public library legislation to date, appeared the same year, paid for by the British Columbia Public Library Commission. (It would be updated and reissued at regular intervals, with supplements in intervening years.) The *Canadian Library Directory, 1947-1948* constituted the third in the reference series. Published biennially with annual supplements, it would later appear in *Canadian Library*. A bio-bibliographical work, *Canadian Biographies: Artists and Authors* (later to include musicians), was issued in loose-leaf form between 1948 and 1952. Among slighter publications, *100 Library Years in Canada, 1851-1951: A Picture Book of Libraries* marked the centenary of the first library legislation in the country.

A series of occasional papers had been proposed as early as 1951, with Jean Lunn's report to the UNESCO conference on "The Bibliographic Situation in Canada" suggested as the first. In fact, the series was not launched until 1953, and Neal R. Harlow's *Bibliographers in an Age of Science*, reprinted from *Le Revue de l'Université d'Ottawa*, constituted No. 1. The same year saw the publication of Verner W. Clapp's analysis of the role of the national library. Subsequent papers in the series were devoted to children's books, library cooperation, the research library, book fairs, and the future of bibliography. No. 8 (1956) provided a basic list of reference books for a small public library in an English-speaking community, and No. 9, issued the same year, summarized a survey of public library salaries and working conditions.

David Foley, in his article on the association's publications, remarked that if it were to adopt a printer's device for its title-pages, the appropriate symbol would be "not a Gutenberg press, but a multilith machine."[34] Except for the *Bulletin*, which was intended to have a public relations function and was printed by letterpress, many of the association's early titles were reproduced from typescript. This was true of the early reference publications and occasional papers, the monthly issues of the *Canadian Index* after the first three years, and *Feliciter* in its initial years. In an era before desktop publishing, the multilith offered both economy and flexibility. A new machine in 1955 "allows shorter runs of publications and decreases storage space. Multilith duplimats are stored in special equipment under subject headings thus making the mats as quickly available as correspondence."[35]

The Campaign for a National Library

One of the resolutions passed at the organizational conference in Hamilton in 1946 had called on the CLA to work towards the establishment of a national library. Like many of CLA's early projects, the campaign for a national library had a long history. Sir John A. Macdonald had suggested the need for such a library in debate over the Library of Parliament in 1883. Lawrence J. Burpee, historian and chief librarian of the Ottawa Carnegie Library, had argued strenuously for a national library in 1911, a fight taken up by the Ontario Library Association, which urged the Laurier government to establish a royal commission. The report of the Commission of Enquiry in 1933 had devoted a chapter to the "need for a national library policy" and had set out the role of a national institution. Seven years later the Royal Commission on Dominion-Provincial Relations had expressed "sympathy with such a project."[36] Felix Desrochers, librarian of Parliament, in his annual report of 1943, had recommended the establishment of a national library, to which books not needed in the overcrowded Library of Parliament could be transferred, and the joint parliamentary committee on the library had agreed. The brief presented by the Canadian Library Council to the Turgeon committee in 1944 had also mentioned the need for a national library.

Following the first meeting of the CLA Council, held in Toronto at the end of October 1946, an informal dinner meeting was arranged with representatives of the Royal Society of Canada, the Canadian Historical Association, the Canadian Institute for International Affairs, and other academics to discuss a national library. An inter-association committee, chaired by Freda Waldon and supported by the provincial library associations and other interested organizations, was established to prepare a brief. The joint brief presented to the government in December set out the functions of a national library, the benefits to be achieved, and "proposals for the first steps in the establishment of the National Library for Canada."[37] The main argument of the brief was that the functions of a national library did not need to wait for a building, that the initial focus should be on services rather than on collections. This, Freda Waldon would later recall, was "the new idea I had added to the long campaign. It came to me as a flash of inspiration but I realized later that the germ of the idea probably came from Madge Gill."[38] This concept was significant because, it was believed, governments had long been put off by the magnitude of the project.

> The Brief therefore asks that a committee be set up to investigate the practical possibilities of beginning the collection and storage of the book stock, and of starting such services as the Brief suggests, namely,
> (1) Coordination of Existing Library Resources,
> (2) National Bibliography,
> (3) National Book Production Displays,
> (4) Technical Services to Libraries,
> *now* in temporary quarters with a suitable staff. In other words the National Library can begin as *an Information Bureau and Bibliographical Centre*, while at the same time, the investigation of the whole question of the ultimate organization of the National Library, its book stock and the building that will be needed to house its collections and its services is continued.[39]

The committee had hoped to present its brief to Prime Minister Mackenzie King, but was referred to the secretary of state, Colin Gibson, with whom they met on 25 January 1947. Gibson was sympathetic to the idea and asked "very penetrating and intelligent questions" of the delegation.[40] At the 1947 CLA conference, C.K. Morison of the British Columbia Public Library Commission proposed that work toward a national library be "the principal objective for this year" and that a standing committee be formed to coordinate efforts.[41] During its first year, the committee was chaired by Freda Waldon, the outgoing president.[42] The association published articles, bombarded members of Parliament and the provincial legislatures with literature, sent out press releases to individuals and organizations, contacted prominent figures, and generally mobilized public opinion. In August 1947 Waldon spoke about the issue on national radio. Among the individuals contacted was Vincent Massey, who, unaware of the CLA's campaign, had spoken to the Canadian Club of Ottawa in 1947 about the work of UNESCO and the role played by national libraries in that organization. The CLA obtained permission to reprint his speech and distribute it widely. Waldon carried on a lengthy correspondence with Colin Gibson and sent him newspaper clippings from across the country. They had established a rapport at their first meeting since both were from Hamilton.

In September 1948, W. Kaye Lamb of the University of British Columbia

Library, who was the outgoing president of the Canadian Library Association, was appointed dominion archivist; at his insistence, he was also given special responsibility for the establishment of a national library.[43] The government also set up a National Library Advisory Committee chaired by Dr Lamb. Two years later the Bibliographic Centre was established, and Martha Shepard was appointed director and Jean Lunn bibliographer. Shepard had been on the staff of the reference department of the Toronto Public Library, where she had worked under Elizabeth Morton. As mentioned, she had also been involved in the CLA microfilming project. She later commented, "I have always felt that it was Elizabeth who suggested my name to Dr. Lamb as a possible candidate for the position at the Bibliographic Centre."[44] The centre took over the *Canadian Catalogue of Books*, which had published annually by TPL for nearly thirty years, and in January 1951 began issuing a national bibliography of current publications, *Canadiana*. Work was begun on a national union catalogue by photographing the card catalogues of major libraries across the country.

Also significant for the founding of a national library was the appointment in 1949 of the Royal Commission on National Development in the Arts, Letters and Sciences, chaired by Vincent Massey. The commission received numerous briefs recommending a national library, including one from the Canadian Library Association. The CLA brief recommended the following: amendment of the Copyright Act to make the National Library the legal depository for all material copyrighted in Canada, reference service to the government and researchers in Ottawa and to any person in Canada through interlibrary loan or photographic reproduction, a centrally located building, a functional design for the building, and a collection focused on books by Canadians or of direct importance to the country.[45] The Massey Commission in its report, published in 1951, acknowledged the efforts made by CLA to draw the issue to the attention of the government. It recommended that "a National Library be established without delay."[46] The passing of the National Library Act, announced at the CLA conference in Banff the following June, was greeted with "general rejoicing."[47] The act came into effect on 1 January 1953. W. Kaye Lamb was appointed national librarian in addition to his position as dominion archivist, and an architectural firm was chosen to prepare plans.

In fact, it would be another fourteen years before the National Library of Canada had a building of its own, and the association would continue to campaign for that goal, but a significant milestone had been reached with the passing of the 1952 act. In summing up the contribution made by CLA, F. Dolores

Donnelly described it as a "planned and co-ordinated national campaign" whose purpose was "the systematic imparting of accurate information to those on whose support the promotion of the National Library issue depended: government ministers and members of Parliament, newspaper editors, representatives of scholarly and other national organizations," in order to "stimulate relevant and informed thinking."[48] Thus when an national library was discussed in the House of Commons and in newspaper articles and editorials, there was an understanding of the issues involved. Of particular importance, in Donnelly's view, was the decision to enrol the support and cooperation of the academic community early in the process, with the result that the CLA was not seen to be acting purely out of self-interest.

"I Love This Work, But ..."

Two other projects in which the CLA was involved in this first decade were the Canadian Book Centre and Young Canada's Book Week. The book centre, established in 1948 and closed two years later, was a joint undertaking of the Canadian Council for Reconstruction through UNESCO (CCRU) and the CLA. Its purpose was to distribute free educational material to libraries and other institutions in postwar Europe. Premises were secured for the centre in Halifax through the federal Department of Public Works and the National Harbours Board. The project had an initial allocation of $50,000 from the CCRU, and approximately a quarter of a million books and periodicals were donated through a "march of books" campaign across the country in a six-month period. The centre's staff of fourteen sorted, listed, and shipped this material overseas as it was requested by institutions in the eight countries selected for aid.

Young Canada's Book Week was launched as a pilot project in Toronto in 1948 and celebrated nationally the following year. The Canadian Association of Children's Librarians organized the event, with assistance from CLA, the publishers' section of the Toronto Board of Trade, and educational and service organizations. Each year a distinguished Canadian was selected to serve as patron. Interest in books was stimulated among children by plays, films, puppets, storytelling, and visits to libraries, and among adults through book fairs, magazine articles, and radio, television, and press publicity.

From the beginning, the central office had been intended as a clearinghouse for library information. As the association became better known, this function required more and more time. In a report to Council in February 1949,

Elizabeth Morton stated that letters going out from the office averaged thirty a day. Queries ranged from information on a national library from a cabinet minister to library services for a bilingual population from the Philippines. To conserve staff time she tried to discourage phone calls, but in one day the office had received the following queries: a request for the address of Columbia University's library school, whether a librarian had been appointed to the Halifax Public Library, whether a friend in the United States who was a librarian could work in Canada during the summer without an immigration work permit, where pictures of children's libraries could be borrowed, and the names of three English-speaking Canadian librarians who were fluent in French and might be willing to work in a northern library.[49] The central office also had major responsibility for organizing the annual conferences. Planning for conferences went on all year. As much work as possible was delegated to local committees; but headquarters staff, particularly the executive secretary, was needed to coordinate activities, give advice, handle registration, and collect and mail out reports, ballots, and other material.

The 1951 conference, held at the University of Toronto, was a time of reappraisal. On the one hand, the executive secretary could point to a number of projects of the Canadian Library Council that were now completed or well under way. Cost accounting and more streamlined record keeping allowed for better evaluation of projects and activities. At the same time, major funding from the Carnegie Corporation was coming to an end, and several projects were not yet self-supporting. Membership fees were now the largest single source of income. The association received grants from several of the provinces that ranged between $2,000 from Ontario and $200 from Prince Edward Island and smaller amounts from the regional library associations. But even with the last instalment of the Carnegie grant to the *Canadian Index*, expenditure surpassed revenue by about $1,000, and money had to be "borrowed" from such capital funds as life memberships. Lack of resources meant the curtailing of certain activities, such as field trips, and the reorganization of projects. As Freda Waldon stated in the report of the planning committee, "We need a larger income even to hold our own."[50] Over the next year the budget and finance committee carried out a major campaign on behalf of the Development and Endowment Fund, with the goal of raising up to $100,000 from corporations and individuals. (In fact, by April 1955 slightly under $30,000 would have been received.) New subscribers were found for the *Canadian Index*. Membership was increased by 12 per cent over the previous year. Nevertheless, finances continued to be problematic. In 1953-54, although "many of our undertakings have been eliminated or cut to the bone," the association had a deficit of $3,185.10 in its general operations,[51] and in 1955 the fee scale was increased for the first time since 1946. But as the treasurer, Robert Blackburn, later recalled, the increase "did not reduce membership as the woe-sayers had predicted it would."[52]

The early program of the CLC had included library visits, funded by the Rockefeller Foundation, and the activities committee of 1946 recommended that they continue. In the early years of CLA, Elizabeth Morton attempted to visit each region of the country every three years as finances allowed. She made trips to the Maritimes in 1948, 1951, and 1954, Quebec in 1952 and 1954 (Montreal was visited annually), Manitoba in 1949 and 1952, and western Canada in 1948, 1950, 1952, and 1955. Ontario centres were visited more irregularly whenever they could be fitted in with other trips. Sometimes these tours were combined with planning for conferences. Sites would be appraised for future gatherings, or Morton would meet with local conveners to discuss arrangements.

In 1983 Mary Morton commented that her sister's involvement with CLA "gave her the opportunity to indulge her fondness for sociability, travel, 'public relations,' new faces, new activities."[53] Certainly she enjoyed these tours of libraries across the country, but they were hard work. Following the Ottawa conference of 1948, for example, she travelled to Fredericton to attend a two-day meeting of the Maritime Library Association. While in New Brunswick, she interviewed the deputy provincial secretary about the provincial library act. She then journeyed overnight to Halifax, where she met with the acting head of the Nova Scotia Library Commission. In that city she also attended meetings of the Canadian Federation of University Women, discussed the microfilming of Nova Scotia newspapers with the provincial archivist, spoke to the Library Club of Halifax, discussed plans for the proposed city library with the architect, visited the Dalhousie University Library, and looked over the Nova Scotian Hotel as a possible site for a conference. She then visited Truro, Moncton (where the public library had recently been destroyed by fire), Saint John (visiting both the public library and the museum, which was lending newspapers for the microfilm project), and McAdam Junction.[54] The trip in all occupied ten days, without benefit of air travel.

These field trips were much appreciated by librarians working in smaller, more isolated communities, who could discuss their problems with her and learn about developments in other parts of the country. Roberta Wilson Weiner recalls a visit when she was working in the Fraser Valley. "A vivid memory: early morning at a tiny railway station near Abbotsford, B.C. A small chuckling woman descending from the train with an NFB carton under her arm. She was bringing 'Library on Wheels,' the film NFB had shot in the Fraser Valley in 1944. We, the staff, were about to see ourselves as stars ... A point that ... ought to be stressed: the isolation of Canadian libraries and librarians before CLA. We did not know each other. EM became the link – she travelled, she observed, she talked, she chuckled, she published those delightful early bulletins of CLC & then CLA."[55]

Tours to study library developments were also made to the United States or, combined with vacations to save money, to Britain and Europe. In November 1948, following a meeting of Council in Winnipeg, Morton visited the Milwaukee Public Library to review its public relations, audio-visual, and young people's operations and then the ALA headquarters in Chicago, where she met with officials in a number of areas. She returned to Ottawa by way of London, Galt, Hamilton, and Toronto. This trip was followed a few days later by a visit to Montreal.[56] It is not surprising that the pace sometimes caught up with her. In the course of a crowded visit to Halifax in 1951, she had to admit, "I overslept the next morning so Mr Detective Grossman [Peter Grossman, director of libraries for Nova Scotia] found me in the Coffee shop at 9:55 a.m."[57]

The field trips also helped to make CLA better known. When a visit to British Columbia was being discussed at a Council meeting in 1955, Willard Ireland commented that something must be done to provide Morton with more help in the office so that the trips could continue. The association had "no better public relations than Miss Morton."[58] Her contacts were wide. From Verner Clapp at the Council on Library Resources in Washington came a note in reply to one from her. "There's not a thing in the hemispheres that escapes the notice of the blessed Elizabeth and the attention of the international Canadian Library Association; and no occasion is so fragile that they don't do something nice about it. May I hope that the same might possibly be some day said of the Council on Library Resources?"[59]

The growing number of projects, sections, and committees put a heavy load on headquarters staff and created the need for more space. Over the years the office moved several times within the building at 46 Elgin Street. By 1955 CLA had a large central office, with four small offices opening off it that accommodated bookkeeping and membership functions, microfilm and multilith equipment, special projects, and the executive secretary. There were three full-time staff members, eleven part-time, and five casual employees, in addition to consultants and those working on commission, such as the advertising agent. The number and make-up of the staff had constantly to be adjusted like a concertina, as one of the presidents expressed it, depending on the workload for a particular year.

Many individuals who knew Elizabeth Morton have commented on her dedication to her work and the skill with which she managed the office. She herself "put in at least an 18-hour work-day; it was well known that she spent evenings and weekends in her office planning, writing and keeping in touch with librarians by telephone ... She was ready to take off at a moment's notice with a brief-case full of papers. She was modest and frugal regarding accommodation – dipping into her own pocket was the rule."[60] A quotation from the *New Yorker* that hung in her office in the 1960s read: "I love this work, but I think that to do it well one should combine the head of a scientist with the heart of an artist, the ingenuity of a used-car salesman with the energy of a marathon runner. There is never any respite."[61] The pace Morton set herself and her characteristic good humour are all the more remarkable when it is remembered that already "in the fifties, she was suffering from painful arthritis ... Her day usually began around 5:30 a.m. with an hour-long soak in the tub, to limber up sufficiently to move about."[62] When the elevator was out of service on weekends and holidays, she had to walk up four flights of stairs to the office.

Throughout her tenure, she economized and made do with the association's limited resources. Catherine Moyse Knowles, who came to the CLA office in 1948, recalls that "we all worked on the assumption that *everything* must be re-used (except postage stamps) with the result that office memos were on small bits of old envelopes, labels, notices, cardboard and stationery. Paper clips and elastic bands were zealously guarded while wrapping paper was kept in service unto the third time – if it could still hang together."[63] In the early days at 46 Elgin Street, "when a visitor called, Miss Ross sat on a roll of wrapping paper which, she pointed out was 'just the right height' for her desk. All money was being conserved for services!"[64]

Morton inspired her staff to work to the best of their abilities. She was "always accessible and fully aware of every facet of work. She visited all offices daily, and kept an eye on things. It was she who established priorities and deadlines, posted daily on the bulletin board."[65] Many of the staff who worked in the office in the early days were married women with young children who worked part time. Morton "put typewriters into homes of those who typed index cards, and maintained a delivery system of magazines to those who did the indexing, thus cutting on rent expenses and enabling many talented people to continue their work."[66] According to Isabel Lee Bradley, who worked at the CLA office in the late 1950s, "when necessary, she permitted flexible hours and working at home, at a time when such practices were virtually unheard of."[67] Some employees worked in the evenings, and printing and packaging were done at night.

Her interest in her employees extended beyond the professional. "She was concerned if one had a place to live, a warm coat for Ottawa's blustery winters, a ride home during a blizzard and ... the proper eyeglasses. A mistake in proofreading could only be explained by faulty vision, and this had to be corrected!"[68] Though she could occasionally show her displeasure and berate an employee, mistakes were quickly forgiven. Most remember only her "bright, cheerful personality, her bubbling sense of humour and her distinctive laugh."[69] It is no wonder that she collected around her "a staff of efficient, congenial, loyal people ... The quality and quantity of work accomplished in cramped quarters with inadequate financial support was amazing."[70] Joyce Sowby summed it up for many who worked in the CLA office under Elizabeth Morton: "Suffice it to say that they were great years."[71]

The Canadian Library Association had come into existence during a remarkable period in the country's history. With the end of the war, Canadians were full of optimism about the future. "There is no doubt that a new life is stirring in Canada. Given a peaceful world we could be on the verge of that great flowering of a distinctive national culture which we have desired for so long."[72] The following decade would see the Massey Commission, the Stratford Festival, the founding of the National Library, and great expansion in many of the country's cultural institutions. The CLA both benefited from and contributed to this era of growth and optimism.

3

Libraries, Librarianship, and Canadian Society: Issues of the Second Decade

The first two objects of the Canadian Library Association, as set out in the constitution of 1947, were "to promote education, science and culture within the nation through library service" and "to promote high standards of librarianship and the welfare of librarians."[1] Standards of library service, librarianship, and library legislation had been included in the second phase of activities proposed at the founding convention in 1946. Much of the work in these areas would be carried out by the numerous committees established by CLA in its first two decades. Though activity began on some issues soon after the 1946 conference, they became increasingly the focus of the association's endeavour in the decade after 1955. The committee on committees in 1959 could point to some thirteen groups working on aspects of the welfare of libraries and fifteen on the welfare of librarians.

The Canadian Library Council's brief to the Turgeon committee in 1944 had addressed the inadequacy of library service in Canada. It drew attention to figures compiled by the Dominion Bureau of Statistics in 1938, which showed that 8 per cent of the population in cities, 58 per cent in towns and villages, and 95 per cent in rural districts were without access to libraries. Yet an expenditure of $1.25 to $1.50 per capita, the council pointed out, would provide adequate service. Little had changed between 1938 and the founding of CLA in 1946. As Freda Waldon recalled, "Libraries were short of staff and books, salaries were shockingly low, and almost no library buildings had been erected during a decade and a half of depression followed by war."[2]

The Canadian Library Association made a beginning in the area of legislation with the publication of *Canadian Public Library Laws, 1946.* Supplements were issued in 1948, 1949, and 1950 and a new compilation in 1953. The committee responsible for legislation had originally intended to analyse its findings. However, because of the great differences in library development across the country, it decided not to attempt a national standard. Instead, to the first supplement the committee appended an eight-page commentary "which assembles the opinions of Canadian librarians on certain questions of major importance."[3] These questions included the advantages of broad versus detailed legislation, the government department versus the library commission, the appointment and make-up of boards, regional libraries, taxation, standards, and the certification of librarians. The committee hoped that the opinions expressed "may prove of practical value to those confronted with legislative problems."[4]

The process of compiling standards in other areas would prove equally difficult. The planning committee in 1951 reported at the annual meeting, "You will be able to think of achievements under every heading of the original Activities Report except in the matter of setting up Library Standards for Canada, though even here the first step has been taken by the publication of Canadian Library Laws in convenient form and Salary Standards for Public Libraries."[5] Four years later, in summing up the first decade, the CLA *Bulletin* could point to progress in some areas. *Suggested Standards of Service for Public Libraries in Canada* had been compiled and would be approved at the annual conference that year. Those relating to cataloguing and reference service were being put together by the sections concerned. In the area of librarianship, standards for positions and salary scales in public libraries had been completed, comparable standards for college and university libraries were being studied, and an evaluation of library education was under way.

A Canadian library charter, or bill of rights, had been proposed at the annual conference in 1951 by the Ontario Library Association. Such a charter would encompass the rights of the Canadian people with regard to library service, the responsibilities of libraries, and the duties of government. The work of composing a charter was entrusted to a committee chaired by Dr Gerhard R. Lomer of McGill University. A revised draft was submitted to the annual conference in 1952, but was referred back to the committee for further work.[6] Perhaps librarians were better at more down-to-earth undertakings because, like attempts to define the purpose and philosophy of librarianship a few years later, this project soon lapsed.

The Welfare of Libraries

The committee on public library standards had been established in 1950 following a panel discussion on the issue at the Winnipeg conference the previous year. A first draft of the committee's proposed standards was reviewed at the 1953 conference, and after some revisions, was accepted as an interim report the following year. With further amendments, the document was approved at the annual meeting in 1955. Work on the project had been delayed by the death in February 1954 of the committee's chair, Ruth E. Cameron of New Westminster, and two Halifax members were forced make the final revisions on their own in order to complete the report in time. In presenting *Suggested Standards of Service for Public Libraries in Canada*, the committee stressed that these were "targets at which to aim, and are not binding rules and regulations."[7] Although the American Library Association's *Post-War Standards for Public Libraries* had provided some guidance, the committee recognized that Canadian conditions were different. Also, as the planning committee had pointed out in 1951, "we have all found that American standards carry very little weight with Canadian governments."[8] The standards recognized the public library's basic purpose as contributing "to the education and to the cultural growth of the community."[9] They made recommendations about the size, composition, and growth of the book collection relative to the population it served; the essentials for adequate service, including a qualified staff, financial support, and efficient administration; and the composition of the library board. The standards were reissued with minor revisions in 1957. Significantly, the word "suggested" had now been dropped from the title. They also appeared in French that year as *Normes de service pour les bibliothèques publiques au Canada*. New standards were published in 1961. The committee on public library standards had in the meantime become a subcommittee of the public libraries committee, established in 1957. Other subcommittees were formed to examine salary standards and statistics.

Difficult as it had been to compile the standards, they were only a beginning. In assuming the presidency in 1955, Willard Ireland had commented, "They will become significant only to the degree that we seek to make them realities, and this will take courage as well as Canadian currency."[10] In 1961 the public libraries committee surveyed public and regional libraries to see how they compared with the minimum standards for their population with regard to income, book stock, and professional staff. It determined that many small libraries still fell below the recommended standards, and of the 35 libraries serving populations over 50,000, only one met the 1957 minimums. Much work remained to be done.

Public library standards underwent a major review in 1963-67. As early as 1957, dissatisfaction with them had been expressed by some large urban libraries, and the 1962-63 committee recommended that they be completely rewritten. The work became a project of the association, financed by personal gifts and interest-free loans from members of Council. A meeting was arranged in October 1963 with Dr Lowell A. Martin, who had chaired the ALA standards committee. He recommended that new standards be based, not on a survey of existing conditions, but on "the knowledge and judgment of a highly respected and experienced group of professional librarians who had consulted and used the advice of experienced laymen."[11] In January 1965, Jane Laird, a graduate student at McGill, was hired to, as Elizabeth Morton reported at Council, "bring order out of the chaos."[12] Morton, Laird, and Alberta Letts, who chaired the standards committee, worked on several drafts of the document. Morton also discussed it with the graduate class at McGill and with librarians during the course of a field trip to western Canada. A draft of the qualitative standards was presented at the annual conference in 1966. It was published the following year, and a French edition appeared in 1968.

Library Buildings. The public library standards of 1955 and 1957 had advised library officials to "keep in touch with current developments in library planning"[13] and had drawn attention to the work of the architecture and building committee. Even before this group had been set up in 1953, CLA had cooperated with the Royal Architectural Institute of Canada in producing a special issue of the institute's *Journal* devoted to libraries in February 1947. Reprinted and distributed by CLA as *Library Buildings for Canada*, the publication contained plans and sketches of recent or planned buildings and articles by Anne Hume, Edgar S. Robinson, R.D. Hilton Smith, Lillian H. Smith, and Freda F. Waldon on aspects of good library design. Under the aegis of the architecture and building committee, a similar issue was produced by the RAIC and CLA in 1959 with the title *Libraries in Canada Today.* It included an annotated bibliography on the planning and construction of library buildings, compiled by the chair of the committee, David C. Appelt.

Other projects undertaken by the committee to promote good library design included an exhibit at the Halifax conference in 1954, a workshop focused on the nearly completed Vancouver Public Library in 1957, and a list of Canadian architects with experience in designing library buildings, which was published as an occasional paper in 1959. After this period of activity, the committee was allowed to lapse in 1961-62, but in response to demand from members, it was reappointed the following year. Workshops, exhibits, and discussions on new or renovated buildings were presented at conferences in the 1960s, and a central file of photographs, plans, and trade catalogues was established at the Kitchener Public Library.

The planning committee of 1951 had recognized that standards for college and university libraries would be "an even more difficult undertaking because of the great variety in the administration, sources of support, functions and specialization of the institutions the libraries serve. It does not seem possible to recommend that this be undertaken in the immediate future."[14] A committee was eventually formed in 1962 to work on standards for academic libraries. A year later this project was transferred to the newly established Canadian Association of College and University Libraries.

By the late 1960s it would seem to pioneers such as Freda Waldon that despite the many problems still facing libraries,

> there has been much progress. All the provinces now have library legislation and library agencies. University libraries have benefited greatly from federal funds. School libraries are, at last, taken seriously by educational authorities. Regional libraries are being developed in nearly every province. New buildings, for both public and academic libraries, were scattered all over Canada even before the Centennial gave added impetus to the movement ...
>
> The Canadian Library Association cannot, of course, take *all* the credit for this improvement ... General economic prosperity has helped, but the stimulation that has come from our national association and its activities, directly and indirectly, has inspired many of these developments.[15]

The Welfare of Librarians

Salaries and Working Conditions. Efforts to improve the welfare of librarians also began early in the association's history. A salaries committee was established in the autumn of 1946, following the organizational conference, "to investigate and report on the salaries and working conditions of librarians in Canada."[16] Two years later the terms of reference were extended to include "personnel administration and welfare." From 1952 the committee functioned as two subcommittees, one devoted to salaries and the other to personnel matters, including job classification and benefits. Members of the committee were chosen to provide a geographical representation, although it was later found more practical to establish a core membership in one place, with consultants in other parts of the country.

The committee in 1948 recommended that separate schedules be devised for university and special libraries, as well as for the smaller public libraries, because "it is very difficult for all the types of libraries in Canada to fit into such a Procrustean bed as the present schedule."[17] Questionnaires had been sent to 144 institutions, predominantly public libraries but including 30 university and 28 special and legislative libraries. With the assistance of a consultant from the Dominion Bureau of Statistics, the committee asked about salaries and bonuses, vacations, sick leave, hours of work, and pensions. A beginning salary for a BLS "fresh from library school" was found to be almost universally $1,800 a year. A "tendency to shorten the working hours of librarians" was noted: the average work week in winter was 38 hours. Practically every library had shorter hours in summer. "An interesting feature, too, is the tendency in libraries to develop a 5-day week."[18] Most libraries had a sick leave plan and a pension scheme. Four weeks' vacation was common.

Schedules from six of the larger institutions, chosen from across the country, were published in the CLA *Bulletin* in January 1950 to give "a lift to all schedule-makers (even possibly to some schedules)," and suggestions about how to arrive at a national standard were requested.[19] A tentative plan was worked out by the committee, but when Claude B. Aubry, deputy head of the Ottawa Public Library, drew up a more comprehensive and detailed scheme, the committee advised its adoption.[20] It was approved at the annual meeting in June 1950, and copies were distributed to library boards, governing bodies of universities, civil service commissions, and school boards. Even as the committee struggled with these initial salary standards, pay scales in the country were changing. Now called "salaries and personnel," the committee presented an interim salary scale for four classes of public libraries in 1953 and a revised scale the following year, together with recommendations regarding annual increments, sick leave, and leave for study or travel.

The results of a questionnaire mailed out in 1955 appeared as an occasional paper, *Public Library Salaries and Welfare*, the following year. In commenting on the returns, the committee sounded what would become a familiar refrain. In all but a very few cases, spending in public libraries was below the $2.50 per capita recommended by the CLA standards committee. "There seems little hope as long as libraries eke out an existence on cheese parings that they will ever be able to pay the salaries to professional staff, to attract suitable personnel or to keep experienced staff. The supply of professional people dwindles. Fewer people go to library schools. More potential librarians enter more lucrative professional fields year after year."[21]

A survey on working conditions in large and medium-sized public libraries, compiled by R.M. Donovan of the Fort William Public Library, was published in the CLA *Bulletin* in November 1958. The information provided for each library included salary ranges, hours of work, holidays, pension and health plans, and the library's policy on conference expenses. With this report was a survey, put together by Jean Eckmeier, of small communities in Huron County, Ontario, which had one of the longest histories of organized county library service in the province. Of these small libraries, Donovan remarked that "there is no evidence of any individual or group plans for hospitalization, medical services or pensions; only one library reported attendance at conferences, with assistance by the Library Board; hourly rates in many instances are startling."[22] Evidently "Working Conditions in Canadian Public Libraries" proved useful since it was reissued in the *Bulletin* and later as a separate publication at regular intervals throughout the 1960s.

Following the establishment of the public library committee in 1957, salary standards for public libraries also became the responsibility of that group. A committee on salaries and personnel in university and college libraries had been formed in 1955, and committees were also set up to examine salaries in special and government libraries. To oversee the work of these groups, a coordinator was appointed in 1958. It was hoped thus to improve liaison between the groups, but they tended to go their own ways. The following year, Council was informed that the university library minimum was $300 higher than that recommended for public libraries. When salary scales for public and university libraries were published together in 1957, the committee on academic libraries stressed that because the educational qualifications for librarians in these institutions "are equivalent to those of many members of the teaching faculty" and the work required "special training and ability," salary standards should be based on those of the faculty.[23] As with standards in academic libraries, salaries and working conditions became the purview of CACUL after it was established in 1963. Its *Draft Report on Position Classification & Salary Scales in Canadian Academic Libraries*, presented to the annual conference in 1966, lamented, "The academic librarian, unlike the librarian off campus, finds himself in an indefensible limbo between faculty and clerical ranks."[24] The suggested guide for librarians' salaries compared categories of librarians with ranks in the teaching staff.

The report spelled out the qualifications, duties, authority, and accountability of six grades of librarians and four grades of clerical and supporting staff, now called library assistants.

Despite taking the lead in establishing salary standards for professional librarians, CLA was sometimes in the embarrassing position of not paying its headquarters staff the recommended minimum. When in 1958 the principle of following the CLA scale for the executive staff was proposed at Council, it was pointed out that the resulting increases in salaries might hamper the association's program and require a reorganization of positions in the office. A year later, Council was informed that $600 would be needed to bring the salaries of three staff members up to the 1956 scale. If the money could not be found, there would be no alternative but to reduce the staff or the program. In 1960 the annual meeting approved an increase of 11 per cent to bring headquarters salaries up to the current standards for public libraries.

Although the committee on salaries had been able to report in 1948 that "nearly every library today has a pension scheme,"[25] six years later it recommended that consideration be given to a national plan. "Librarians would like to move from province to province as it is possible to do under the ALA pension scheme."[26] Discussions were begun with insurance companies, and several were invited to submit proposals. The result was a retirement plan for members of CLA that was endorsed at the annual meeting in 1958. As described in a pamphlet sent out with *Feliciter* that November, it provided two plans, one for employees without pension provision or the self-employed and the other for individuals whose employer was a member of CLA. Two years after its inauguration, the scheme could report thirteen employer-employee groups under plan B and seventeen individuals enrolled under plan A. The pension plan committee, originally established to investigate the scheme, had been given responsibility for publicizing it. But the committee had to admit in 1961 that initial results "have been disappointing ... more active participation by the members generally in the promotion of the plan is desirable."[27]

Tenure. Of great importance to the welfare of librarians was the question of tenure. Several cases came before the CLA Council in the 1950s and 1960s. The association continued the policy established by the Canadian Library Council of not taking part in disputes unless requested to do so. Resolutions passed at annual conferences identified "the principle at issue ... rather than the locality."[28] One case was that of John M. Marshall in 1954. Marshall, who had been working with the Fraser Valley Regional Library in Abbotsford, was invited in the fall of 1953 to apply for the position of bookmobile librarian by the Victoria Public Library Board. He was accepted for the job and began work on 1 December. However, at a regular meeting in late January 1954, the board decided not to retain Marshall's services. Though he was told that, because he was still on probation, he had no right of appeal, a public hearing was held by the incoming board in February, which confirmed the previous decision. "Mr. Marshall was never accused of anything by any members of the Library Board, all of whom disclaimed responsibility for the press reports which linked the non-confirmation of his appointment with a connection with Communist organizations."[29]

CLA's inter-library association liaison committee supported the British Columbia Library Association in its investigation of the case. The issue was complicated for the CLA by the fact that both Marshall and the Victoria Public Library Board were members of the association. It was referred to the resolutions committee, and in June the annual meeting passed a resolution stating, "That sound personnel procedures necessarily imply that employment or dismissal of any person shall be based only upon competence to perform the professional and technical duties involved and that any personal beliefs or actions become pertinent only when it is established that they interfere with the quality of service rendered, professional ethics, or obligations as a citizen."[30] Behind the scenes, the association assisted Marshall by paying him to compile a bibliography of Canadian children's literature.[31] Elizabeth Morton later wrote about the association's position on tenure in the CLA *Bulletin*. Each case, she stated, "is different. Each demands handling with legal precision, imagination and humanity."[32] Marshall and John H. Archer, who was a member of Council at the time, would later agree that "CLA policy was sound for the times and ... Elizabeth handled the subject well."[33]

Two years later, in 1956, the Council reviewed the case of Claire Godbout of Trois-Rivières, whose position of *bibliothécaire en chef* had been abolished so that another individual with the title *conservateur de bibliothèque* could be hired in her place. She was offered employment as a cataloguer, with a decrease in salary, and notification of the change was handed to her on the day a reception was held for the incoming *conservateur*. At the annual conference in Niagara Falls that year, CLA passed a lengthy resolution on security of tenure in which it deplored "the action of this administrative authority for a violation of sound personnel practice" and reaffirmed

> its stand that sound library personnel practice involves the acceptance of the Standards of Service for Public Libraries in Canada as adopted by the Association at its Tenth Annual Conference, 1955, wherein it is stated that, in addition to the qualifications required for

a professional librarian in a public library, the chief librarian shall also have the following qualifications:

(a) Specialized training and experience in their particular fields of service;
(b) Familiarity with the principles and practice of library service;
(c) Thorough knowledge of the social, educational, and industrial characteristics of their communities;
(d) Ability to make library services and resources known throughout the community and recognized as an important contribution to community life.[34]

Because the case turned on the difference between *bibliothécaire* and *conservateur* and the Canadian Press accepted releases only in English, CLA prepared a French version of its announcement about the case to send to French-language newspapers. Of this occasion, Robert Blackburn later recalled "the Council spending a long evening session in a sweltering room overlooking Niagara Falls, wrestling with pleas from two of our members to help them get justice after having suffered improper dismissal ... there was no direct action we could take because the two (one in the northwest, one in the east) had already resigned."[35]

Education and Recruitment. Education for librarianship and recruitment to the profession were also important issues addressed by the association in its first two decades. A recruitment committee was established in 1952 to advertise librarianship as a career. "Among the reasons suggested for the insufficient number of librarians, were," it reported, "the general level of salaries and particularly the maximum salaries, which are not comparable with those of other professions; the fact that there is little security for librarians in some areas; the belief that there is no future in the profession for enterprising and ambitious individuals."[36] The major project of this committee was a nine-minute documentary film entitled *The Librarian*, produced by Crawley Films in 1957 using a script written with the assistance of a group of Ottawa librarians.[37] A strikingly good-looking young man, Tom Lawrence, "discovers" the profession while he is a college student. Miss Abbott, the college librarian, persuades him that because he loves science, books, and people, he would make an excellent librarian. It is a rich and satisfying field with a wide range of career choices. After he has attended library school, Tom is shown joining the staff of the "Queensfort Public Library," where we are introduced to Miss Miller, the chief librarian, Robert Kelly, in charge of technical processes, Mr Patterson, assistant reference librarian, and professionals in charge of children's services and the bookmobile.

The film was shot at Carleton College (as it was then called) and the south branch of the Ottawa Public Library. The recruitment committee prepared a series of leaflets based on the film, and a special issue of the CLA *Bulletin* devoted to recruitment appeared in April 1957 to coincide with the film's release. A French commentary for the film was published in 1958. CLA's excursion into film making began and ended with *The Librarian.* The film had been intended as the first in a series, but the cost of production was high and sales – despite endorsements such as one from Susan Faudi, film librarian at the St Louis Public Library, who described the film as "the very best one on library recruitment that we have seen"[38] – were disappointingly low. No other films were produced.

The CLA Council had discussed the accreditation of library schools in Canada as early as 1947. A resolution had been passed at the annual conference that year that, until the association could set up its own board, it would accept accreditation by the board of education for librarianship of the American Library Association. During the Council's review of the issue, one member suggested a motivation other than cost for not establishing a separate board: "It was pointed out that possible hostility between CLA and unaccredited library schools would be avoided if the ALA rules were observed."[39]

The Halifax conference of 1954 had as its theme a well-known line from Robert Burns, "To see ourselves as others see us." Education for librarianship was a major focus of the conference. As the result of a request from the Ontario Department of Education that CLA consider undertaking the evaluation of Canadian library schools, the question of accreditation was discussed at length at a meeting of Council in June that year. Elizabeth Morton proposed that Dorothy Chatwin, editor of the *Canadian Index*, be given the assignment of collecting material for an evaluation of library training. Chatwin presented her *Investigation Report on Library Education* a year later. In her view, accreditation would be an expensive undertaking for the association, requiring a minimum annual budget of $10,000, including salaries for a full-time secretary (a professional librarian) and a stenographer and travel expenses for the secretary and a board of three to five members. The report recommended that CLA continue the policy established in 1947 of accepting ALA accreditation; this recommendation was modified at the annual meeting to read, "That until 1960, or such time as the situation demands," ALA accreditation be accepted.[40] The report also proposed that CLA take up the question of Canadian representation on the standards committees of the ALA board of education for librarianship.

Though the issue of Canadian accreditation would be raised from time to time in the future, most members who were active in this period believe that the association was right not to set up its own board, "not mainly on grounds of expense, but of credibility ... no Canadian committee could resist regional pressures, or fail to find some way of accrediting every Canadian school that applied ... Better to have an external accrediting body in which the three visitors always had one Canadian member (for US schools) and usually two for Canadian schools."[41] Bruce Peel, who later served as Canadian representative on the ALA committee, "was always opposed for practical reasons to creating a Canadian committee: (1) Too few library schools, so that the staff involved in the process would end up washing each other's linen ... (2) Cost to CLA ... (3) While Canadian standards for library education differed a lot from those of the U.S.A. we benefitted by being attached to their process." His own experience with the ALA committee he remembered as "a highlight in my career as a librarian."[42]

As a result of the Chatwin report, a committee had been established in 1955 "to advance the interests of librarianship through the maintenance and improvement of standards in education for librarianship, through the study of problems and needs in library education, and through the study of personnel problems."[43] The report was published as the first in a series entitled Education for Librarianship. Other publications in the series examined education for school librarians (1957) and British library education (1958). The committee organized a workshop on the subject at the 1958 annual conference, whose proceedings appeared as the fourth in the Education for Librarianship series. In preparation, the April issue of the CLA *Bulletin* that year was devoted to the topic of library education.

Professional Qualifications. Certification for librarians had been introduced by British Columbia in 1944, the first province to do so. Ontario had followed two years later. The Canadian Library Association established a committee in 1955 to "prepare national standards of certification for librarians in Canada."[44] In 1959, in response to a resolution at the annual conference proposed by this committee, the Council passed a motion that no one would be recognized by the association as a fully qualified librarian "unless he holds the equivalent of the B.A. degree as granted in Canada plus proof of library training equivalent to that required for the Bachelor of Library Science Degree (B.L.S.) in Canada or Master of Library Science Degree (M.L.S.) in the United States of America." The association would continue to welcome librarians from abroad, but they "should be fully aware of the Canadian Library Association – Association Canadienne des Bibliothèques position and should be prepared either to accept positions within these limitations or to take further general and professional education to meet these standards."[45] The committee published a pamphlet, *Information on the Certification of Librarians*, in 1961, but certification remained a provincial issue. After a few years the committee was discharged, and CLA did not pursue a national standard.

Within Canada, the association monitored important library positions and on occasion, censured the appointment of non-qualified individuals. In 1955, amendments to the Library of Parliament Act raised the question of what appointments might be made to that institution. It was a particularly difficult issue since the most senior positions were filled by the cabinet. The conference that year passed a resolution endorsing the principle enunciated in a letter sent by the CLA president to the prime minister that "both the Parliamentary Librarian and the Associate Parliamentary Librarian should possess administrative ability and professional competence," including "demonstrated ability in the administration of a large library" and "high standing in the library profession."[46] The issue would be raised again in 1968, with the appointment of Guy Sylvestre to succeed Kaye Lamb as national librarian. Not all members of the association, however, agreed with the public censuring of the appointment at the annual conference that year in the presence of the appointee.

On the recommendation of the salaries and personnel committee, a librarians committee was formed in 1956 to "study the advisability of forming a professional librarians' section within the CLA which would advocate the requirement of professional competence for professional positions, ... implement recruitment, raise the status of the profession of librarianship and encourage growth within it, ... and give support to librarians who work in provinces where few are employed."[47] A number of younger librarians felt that "sufficient is not being done to improve professional standards, status and welfare by C.L.A. or the provincial library associations."[48] Stimulus was also provided by the actions of the Ontario Library Association, which in 1958 would form the Institute of Professional Librarians of Ontario, and by the British Columbia Library Association, which had set up a committee to study problems of professional librarianship.

Three CLA subcommittees examined the questions of purpose, philosophy, and a code of ethics for the profession, but they were frustrated by a lack of response from the membership. The subcommittee on the philosophy of librarianship was forced to report that only nine answers had been received to a questionnaire distributed to all members of the association in the fall of 1957, and it was "impossible to develop a meaningful statement of a philosophy of librarianship from such a paucity of material, although the Committee firmly believed that such a statement was desired by a majority of the profession."[49] Although all three subcommittees recommended fuller studies of their subjects, they were discharged after a year. The librarians committee, however, did propose the establishment of a professional section within CLA. These issues seemed to lapse briefly after the initial enthusiasm of the 1950s, but they would be revived a decade later.

That not all members of CLA were happy with this collective soul searching is evident from a letter written to Elizabeth Morton in November 1958 by Bernard Ower, head librarian at the Dominion Bureau of Statistics. "Get set for a tornado!" it begins.

I do not know why it is that librarians in the last few years have got sudden urges to produce all sorts of inspirational statements. At the Quebec Conference we were served with several hasty puddings dished up by Committees on the purposes and philosophy of librarianship, and we all sat there like stuffed dummies accepting the masses of verbiage presented to us. I was strongly moved to protest the value of these statements, but hated to spoil the serene atmosphere of the Conference. Furthermore, the Chairman banged the gavel down and passed the reports without asking for comments from the floor. If I am at the Conference in Edmonton in 1959, I do not propose to accept this sort of stuff without a protest.

We are now rewarded with our latest horror: The Librarians Professional Credo, Part I. Will the authors of all this nonsense please make a statement as to the purpose and value of all this? Is it to hang on the wall, teach library school students, or in the true meaning of the word credo, to be recited several times a day? Or can it be that the authors consider that most librarians' conduct is so bad that they need a credo to remind them of correct conduct? ...

This credo looks as if it was either written by a library board chairman looking for meek and docile librarians or by some librarian who has become exasperated by the frailties of his brethren. It needs to indicate more of the distinctive attributes of librarianship as a profession and less the general weaknesses of human beings ...

My own view for what it is worth is that a person who has a sense of professional integrity and responsibility doesn't need a credo to remind him of it, and for those lacking such a sense, all the credos in the world won't help.[50]

Recruitment, qualifications, education and training, and the deployment of staff eventually became the purview of a more broadly based committee on education for library manpower, established in 1967. The training of library assistants, or technicians, as they were now called, had become a major concern in the 1960s, and this committee looked at training and qualifications for both professional and non-professional staff. Accreditation, recruitment, and scholarships, previously the focus of separate committees, became subcommittees of the new body. The appropriate use of professional staff was now to be viewed in relation to that of technicians, many of them graduates of programs at community colleges. While some librarians saw these technicians as a threat to their profession, for others they were the answer to the shortage of librarians brought about by the rapid growth of libraries in the 1960s. In his acceptance speech on assuming the presidency in 1965, William Castell pointed out that in many libraries "the ratio of clerical help to professional staff is at least 5 to 1, and that ratio is not going to get better for some time to come. I think it is only common sense if we are going to depend so greatly on non-professional help that we should at least try to get the best. And this can only be done by proper training."[51]

The decade of the 1960s was one of turmoil for the association and the profession, as we shall see in a later chapter; but as it ended, CLA's first president found much to praise. "In Canada there are now three accredited library schools, three more working towards that desirable goal, and all with larger classes than ever before. Two other schools will open soon. Librarians' salaries seem astronomical to those who remember the salaries of the 1930's. Today no young librarian would accept the working conditions many of us endured. While it is still possible for totally unqualified persons to be employed as 'librarians,' advertisements now clearly show that governments and industry are increasingly aware of the value of professional training. Seven of the first twenty-two presidents of our Association have been given honorary degrees by Canadian universities."[52] The profession had come a long way in twenty years.

Speaking Out: The Association as Government Lobbyist

An important function of the Canadian Library Association was to serve as lobbyist with the federal government over issues that concerned libraries and librarians. In 1950-52 Kathleen R. Jenkins had formed a one-person committee to work towards the abolition of sales tax and duty on books. She met in October 1950 with D.C. Abbott, the minister of finance, to present the views of the association. However, the federal budget the following April increased the tax from 8 to 10 per cent, with no exemption for books, and she was forced to report to the annual meeting in 1951 that "one fact has become increasingly clear: *taxation on books, being paid at the wholesale level, is hidden taxation* – most individual book buyers do not know that it exists and therefore cannot be expected to protest."[53] She could only look to the report of the Massey Commission, which was expected shortly and did indeed recommend the removal of the tax on books, and to forthcoming international meetings on tariffs.

From 1952 the CLA had the support of the Canadian Retail Booksellers Association and the publishers' section of the Toronto Board of Trade in a new approach to the minister of finance. This reinforcement had come about through a new standing committee on library-publisher relations, established to consider problems of mutual concern. In the 1953 federal budget, "through the combined efforts of CLA, other educational and cultural organizations, and Canadian publishers," the sales tax on books was abolished and minor changes were made to the customs tariff to allow certain materials to be imported free.[54] Other joint projects of the library-publisher committee in the 1950s included lobbying the federal government to reclassify books to second class for freight rates and to equalize postal rates across the country for books and periodicals, agreement on standardized ordering procedures, and the establishment of a central jobbing agency – the Co-operative Book Centre of Canada – in 1954.

In the course of the Council's fall meeting in 1960, interviews were arranged with federal ministers and government officials on a number of issues. The Council urged the government to extend library postal rates to places served by air stages and to support libraries as educational institutions with regard to exemptions from the federal sales tax on equipment and furniture. When members of Council met with an official of the Department of Finance over the latter issue, he recommended that the association include a definition of a public library with its request for an amendment to the sales tax legislation. Elizabeth Morton attempted to come up with a satisfactory definition, but this proved to be a frustrating exercise. None of the provincial acts defined libraries, and two drafts sent to members of Council were each turned down.

In 1963 the association presented a brief to the Royal Commission on Taxation asking that the sales tax be removed from library equipment, bookmobiles, and other essentials. The 1950s and 1960s were an era of royal commissions. As Bothwell, Drummond, and English remark in *Canada since 1945*, both Conservative and Liberal governments loved them. No less than sixty-four were appointed during CLA's first quarter century, and many had relevance for libraries and librarians. Among those to which the association made representation were royal commissions on Canada's economic prospects (Gordon) in 1955-57, broadcasting (Fowler) in 1955-57, publications (O'Leary) in 1960-61, bilingualism and biculturalism in 1963-70, and the status of women in 1967-70.[55] These briefs were handled in various ways. Sometimes a committee could work at leisure in putting together a document. In the case of the O'Leary commission, councillors who attended the meetings in November 1960 were divided into four groups to prepare a presentation in the course of one day. For the brief to the Royal Commission on Bilingualism and Biculturalism in 1964, two committees were formed, one in Montreal and the other in Ottawa. Elizabeth Morton prepared a draft concerning the CLA and its projects and activities to emphasize its bilingual and bicultural program, while Father Edmond Desrochers provided an analysis of the ways in which libraries contributed to the country's dual character. Ironically, this brief was prepared at a time when CLA's status as a bilingual organization was being challenged (as we shall see in chapter 5).

Occasionally the executive office had to pull things together. Marion C. Wilson recalls that the brief to the Royal Commission on the Status of Women, prepared by a particularly eager member of Council, arrived only a day or two before the deadline.

> It was rambling, anecdotal and was mostly a recital of personal grievances. It was not in any way suitable as a brief from CLA. Elizabeth [Morton] asked me to rewrite it and I did. We had no research facilities in the office and in any case there was no time to make a serious study of the status of women as that related to libraries and librarians. So I did the best I could. I don't think the brief was all that great but it was submitted on time and Elizabeth sent me to speak to it when open hearings were held ... This episode underlines a serious and ongoing problem at CLA in those days. We had a fairly adequate clerical staff but a marked shortage of professional staff and an almost complete lack of research capacity. Elizabeth operated the headquarters on a shoestring and we often took on more than we could handle with anything like ease. Our reach often exceeded our grasp. But maybe that was the secret of CLA's many accomplishments![56]

The brief to the Fowler commission on broadcasting was written by Freda Waldon and Robert Blackburn, and presented to the commission by a delegation led by Blackburn. It drew attention to librarians' interest in broadcasting as a stimulus to reading and a powerful ally "in the task of providing the people of

Canada with information, education, and recreation."[57] When the commission's report was published in 1958, the association made a point of endorsing its recommendations. CLA was "emphatically in favour of the present system of broadcasting in Canada," and it approved "the principle of non-sponsored programmes in the public interest" and favoured "the broadening of the financial base of the Canadian Broadcasting Corporation as that body is presently constituted."[58] Blackburn, who was involved with other briefs to royal commissions, later commented, "I think these particular activities ... were useful to formulate and declare a CLA point of view in matters related to our mission."[59]

Copyright was an issue that directly affected libraries in a number of ways. When the Royal Commission on Patents, Copyright, Trade Marks, and Industrial Design was appointed in 1954 under the direction of J.L. Ilsley, the association was invited to present a brief. But since it was "the view of our members that the control of the relationship of copyright and library service under the existing sections 17(2) and 28(3) of the present Copyright Act 1952 has aided the free flow of knowledge and the competent administration of library service in Canada" and CLA was not requesting a change, the association sent a letter outlining "the present state of library service as affected by the provisions of the Copyright Act and a statement of our policy regarding liaison with groups supplying library materials."[60] In its letter, the association stated that Canadian libraries had benefited from the provisions of the Copyright Act, "which provides for fair practice as to the copying of materials for the purposes of study and research." It could also draw attention to its "free and frank discussion of mutual problems with publishers, publishers' agents, booksellers, film producers and distributors, library supply and equipment firms."[61] At the annual conference in 1955, a resolution was passed stating that "the clauses of the Copyright Act dealing with importation of books by libraries etc., should not be changed." The executive was authorized to take "such further action" with respect to the Ilsley commission "as they feel may be necessary."[62]

When the commission's report on copyright was tabled in the House of Commons in June 1958, the annual conference, meeting in Quebec City a few days later, strongly endorsed its recommendations since the report provided "acceptable procedures for libraries in regard to the importing of printed materials" and allowed "for protection against the infringement of copyright by personal action."[63] The CLA Council decided to establish a committee to monitor any legislation resulting from the report. No committee was appointed until 1959, and after a few years it apparently became inactive. However, the proliferation of photocopy machines in the 1960s revived the issue for Canadian libraries. A resolution at the 1966 conference urged that, since "the Copyright Act which governs the reproduction of copyright material and hence governs the use of such machines is neither clearly enough enunciated nor widely enough understood,"[64] CLA should established a small ad hoc committee to examine the issue. The new group was chaired by Harry Campbell of the Toronto Public Library and including Marsh Jeanneret from the University of Toronto Press. Following the presentation of its report on fair dealing in Canadian library copying, the annual conference in 1967 resolved that the CLA Council "consider keeping a committee on Copyright to work to secure liberalization [of the act], and to devise means of assistance to libraries having problems with copyright."[65] The work of this body was subsequently transferred to the committee on legislation.

INTELLECTUAL FREEDOM

For CLA, the issue of intellectual freedom had grown out of public concerns about obscenity in the early 1950s.[66] A committee on undesirable literature had prepared a brief to the senate committee considering "the Sale and Distribution of Salacious and Indecent Literature."[67] The brief warned that censorship could be a "dangerous instrument which must be handled with the utmost caution and skill." The current method of banning books in Canada it found "disturbing." The "most effective means of combatting the bad book is by substituting the good book."[68] Soon after, this committee appears to have become moribund. But when, in 1958, the association passed a strongly worded statement opposing recent proposals to incorporate a definition of obscenity in the Criminal Code because such a definition "might tend to limit freedom of inquiry,"[69] a new committee was established. At the recommendation of this group, the focus was changed in 1961 to the larger question of intellectual freedom. John Archer chaired the reformulated committee between 1962 and 1966. It began a program of information directed at both libraries and the general public through a series of articles published in *Canadian Library*, beginning with the American Library Association's "The Freedom to Read" and "Library Bill of Rights." So broad was this approach that in 1962 the association's legal adviser pointed out that in his opinion the committee's activities were not in line with its terms of reference. In reply, Archer stated that when he had taken over the committee, he had determined to spend a year preparing good publicity for the issue before proceeding to a statement on censorship.[70]

The articles culminated with Archer's statement "This Freedom," published in *Canadian Library* in March 1963. The second phase of the committee's activities was the drafting of a more formal statement on intellectual freedom. Professor Frank Scott of McGill University wrote the English text for this statement, and Claude Aubry prepared the French version. A pre-conference workshop on issues surrounding intellectual freedom was held at Calgary in 1966, and the statement was approved by the membership that year. It declared:

> Intellectual Freedom comprehends the right of every person (in the legal meaning of the term), subject to reasonable requirements of public order, to have access to all expressions of knowledge and intellectual creativity, and to express his thoughts publicly. Intellectual Freedom is essential to the health and development of society. Libraries have a primary role to play in the maintenance and nurture of intellectual freedom.[71]

In support of these principles, the Canadian Library Association affirmed several specific propositions: that libraries had a responsibility to facilitate the right of access by acquiring and making available a wide variety of material, "including those expressing and advocating unconventional or unpopular ideas"; that they should resist all attempts to limit the exercise of that responsibility; and that librarians had a professional duty to uphold the principles enunciated in the statement. A "watch and ward" committee headed by the immediate past president was established to monitor all matters pertaining to intellectual freedom in Canada.

Though arrived at through a different process a number of years later and expressed in a broader philosophical context, this statement was in some ways the charter of library rights that had been proposed in the early 1950s. It defined the place of libraries and librarians in Canadian society, a society derived "from a rich and varied racial, religious and cultural heritage."[72]

4

Twenty Years A-Growing: The Association in the Mid-1960s

The Canadian Library Association's contribution to society was recognized in 1958 by an award from the Canadian Citizenship Council for "keeping the more durable printed word at the disposal of the Canadian people."[1] The gift of a beaver skin from the citizenship council posed a dilemma for the association. A photograph of the trophy appeared on the cover of the September *Bulletin*, but what to do with it? As Elizabeth Morton reported in a letter to Council, CLA owed a debt to Jean-Charles Bonenfant, legislative librarian for the province of Quebec, for organizing the conference in Quebec City that year. "It was, therefore, decided to present the Beaver Skin to Madame Bonenfant to be made into a hat. Madame Bonenfant's hats had greatly brightened the Conference, and the Beaver Skin was of a colour to enhance her beauty. A resolution from the Directors was forwarded with the Beaver Skin, with the suggestion that if enough fur remained after making the hat that a beaver bow-tie might be contrived for Jean-Charles himself." Yolande Bonenfant replied, expressing her "sheer delight" at the gift.

> Jason was not prouder of his "toison d'or" than I, of this superb beaver pelt. And a hat it will become as the President resolved – and there will be enough left for a bow-tie for Monsieur! ...
>
> Please hold your 14th conference in winter time so that your members may see how a librarian's wife looks under a National Citizenship Award![2]

The Eagle and the Beaver: Montreal, 1960

Alas, no conference was ever held in wintertime. June continued to be the favoured month. A highlight of the association's second decade was the

Montreal conference of 1960, which was held jointly with the American Library Association. Although Elizabeth Morton described CLA's function as primarily that of hospitality, this conference was an extraordinary undertaking for the Canadian organization, given their relative sizes (of the approximately 4,800 delegates, 831 were Canadians).[3] Planning had begun nearly ten years earlier. On 1 March 1960, a office was opened at the Laurentian Hotel in Montreal under the direction of Sheila Egoff to "co-ordinate, consolidate, disseminate."[4] The Canadian staff was joined in April by Mary Cilluffo from the ALA executive offices. That month, ALA published a special number of its *Bulletin* devoted to Canadian libraries and librarianship. Elizabeth Morton contributed an article on the differences between the two national organizations. Kaye Lamb wrote about the National Library, Guy Roberge about the National Film Board, Ian C. Wees about early libraries in Quebec City and Montreal, and Edmond Desrochers about library education in Canada. Short articles about the CLA and ALA-CLA liaison had also appeared in the November 1959 number of *Stechert-Hafner Book News*, published in New York. The March 1960 issue of *Canadian Library* was devoted to ALA and American libraries, and the May issue to Canadian literature, art, films, periodicals, cartography, and broadcasting.

The CLA annual general meeting was held on the day preceding the conference to allow delegates to attend as many sessions as possible of the joint gathering. The banquet that evening was open to members of ALA and visiting librarians from other countries. Two anniversaries were celebrated: sixty years since the founding of the first library association – the OLA – in Canada and the fifteenth year of CLA. An auction of Canadiana raised $600 for the association's scholarship fund. "Overwhelming" was how many Canadians described the joint conference that followed. The proceedings published by ALA in ninety-seven pages of small print consist almost entirely of the reports of the numerous American "type-of-library" divisions and their many committees and subsections. Only in the three general sessions and the brief account of the CLA annual meeting are Canadians evident, though many were involved in planning joint workshops and other meetings.

In reviewing the conference at the November Council meeting, Sheila Egoff pointed to the high cost to CLA in giving up staff time and projects. According to Elizabeth Morton, the sections and some of the committees "missed a whole year in their work."[5] The past president, Bertha Bassam, acknowledged that a joint conference "would interfere more with the regular work of our

Association than it would with the ALA because the ALA is so big and has a much larger executive staff to do the work for the sections ... our staff were struggling to carry on as much as they could with their own work and at the same time give every ounce to putting the conference across. That is why the organization was so good."[6] It was decided to establish an evaluation committee which was asked to recommend whether future joint conferences were desirable. In its interim report, presented to Council in January, the committee concluded that because of the "cost in time and effort, possible financial loss and the considerable disruption of the CLA activities," ten years was a suitable interval between joint conferences. As to whether the conference was "worth it to the CLA as a whole," the committee felt that "most of the opinions expressed are either qualified, or largely in the negative; hardly one is outright in favour." The theme, "Breaking Barriers," had promised "a solution of various problems, particularly those of an international and professional nature. That limited promise was not fulfilled in any substantial respect."[7]

Freda Waldon, writing in 1968, described the joint conference as one of "the proudest achievements of the Canadian Library Association ... Our Association was proud of our President, Bertha Bassam, who presided with characteristic dignity and humour, and we were pleased with the grace and charm of Montreal hospitality. A conference of such size put a strain on the small headquarters staff and on Montreal librarians. Association business was somewhat held back by the special claims of that year, but the success of the conference delighted everyone."[8] Nearly thirty later, opinion is still divided. Robert Blackburn remembers being "overwhelmed by the size of it, frustrated by the overlapping of meetings I wanted to attend, and missing most of them because I could not find the place. The planning looked good, but execution in that Eagle-Beaver context gave the eagle an over-riding claim to all it surveyed. It was not a worthwhile undertaking for me or, I think, for CLA."[9] Neal Harlow, the incoming president in 1960, regretted that he had not "tried to shift some of the financial burden to ALA's broader shoulders."[10] On the other hand, Dean W. Halliwell, although he felt "somewhat overpowered by the number of attendees and meetings," believed the conference "was worthwhile both in opening American eyes to the existence of CLA and in reinforcing Canadian librarians in a belief in their ability (which, being Canadians, they often doubted) to identify, tackle and resolve professional questions as effectively as their American cousins did."[11] Martha Shepard, too, feels that the conference "was a success in that it made some of the ALA members aware of CLA aims and problems. I remember one man saying to me that he was amazed at how witty the Canadian speakers were. What do you suppose he expected?"[12]

Projects of the Second Decade

The major project of the association in the year following the Montreal conference of 1960 was the wide-ranging "program of inquiry," designed to survey "the present state of library service in Canada." It was the brain child of the new president, Neal Harlow. In announcing the project to the membership, he pointed out,

> Not since 1946 has there been an attempt to look at the library resources of Canada as a whole. Then, the Canadian Library Association – Association Canadienne des Bibliothèques – chose as a theme for its first conference, "Libraries in the Life of the Canadian Nation," and in preparation sought information about library facilities from all the provinces. Since those post-war years (when librarians' salaries began at $1,400 a year) many changes have taken place, but we have not systematically noted what they are nor judged whether they are suitable, adequate, sufficiently well supported, or are being extended rapidly enough in the right directions.
>
> In 1960/61, therefore, the CLA – ACB proposes to devote its efforts to finding what our existing library resources are. We shall be concerned with all forms of library service, in every type of library and geographic area; and it is hoped that the provincial and local library associations as well as sections and committees of the national body will take part ... The objective is to discover what the present state of library service is in Canada in order that we can ably plan its subsequent development.[13]

The participating groups were asked a series of questions about the state of service in their area: what statistical data was available; what quantitative standards existed; what goals or objectives had been formulated; a summary statement about library facilities in the area; any methods found useful in reaching the current levels of service; and any specific recommendation for action, to be incorporated into a national plan to improve library service in Canada. The reports were presented in unsynthesized form to the 1961 conference at St Andrews, New Brunswick. After a week in which the findings and recommendations were thrashed out by individual sections and committees and in general session, a series of resolutions was passed. The conference agreed that work was needed in several areas: federal aid, statistics, standards, school library service, the shortage of librarians, the National Library, and a long-range program.

It was soon realized that the inquiry, originally conceived as a one-year project, would have implications far beyond that year. A planning and action committee, chaired by Father Desrochers, was formed in 1961 to assess the findings of the inquiry. It prepared a five-year plan for library service (1962-67) and identified seventeen areas of priority. These were assigned to specific sections or standing committees of CLA. The planning and action committee organized workshops on government aid to libraries – considered to be crucial if they were to meet the greatly increased demand for service anticipated in the future – at the 1962 and 1963 conferences and was involved in planning the twentieth-anniversary conference, held in Toronto in 1965. At the recommendation of the planning and action committee, a committee was established to prepare briefs to the National Library on a regular basis.

The passing of the National Library Act in 1952 had seemed the culmination of a long campaign. But as the years passed, a building for the library was repeatedly postponed. Services which the National Library should have been providing were hampered or curtailed. Frustration over the delays increased. When no funds for a building appeared in the Public Works estimates in the spring of 1959, the CLA, together with the learned societies that had launched the campaign for a national library in 1946, prepared a brief to Prime Minister John Diefenbaker. In the course of Council meetings in November 1959, a delegation met with the prime minister, who was reportedly interested in the issue and who expressed comments and took notes. The annual conference in 1960 passed a resolution that CLA "draw to the attention of the Prime Minister and the Members of Parliament the repeated postponement of the construction of the building for the National Library, express our dismay that no action has yet been taken and ask that funds will be appropriated in the 1961-62 Budget for an immediate start on the building programme."[14]

A new campaign was launched, with letters, articles, and a pamphlet, *And Canada's National Library*, which reprinted articles by H. Pearson Gundy and Kaye Lamb. The design on the cover, originally used on the CLA *Bulletin* in February 1947, enumerated in continuous lines of type the countries worldwide that had national libraries:

algeria has a national library argentina has a national library australia has a national library austria has a national library brazil has a national library bulgaria has a national library chile has a national library czechoslovakia has a national library denmark has a national library ethiopia has a national library france has a national library guatemala has a national library iran has a national library ireland has a national library peru has a national library poland has a national library russia has a national library scotland has a national library siam has a national library sweden has a national library switzerland has a national library south africa has a national library united states of america has a national library uruguay has a national library venezuela has a national library wales has a national library.

CLA president Neal Harlow and Council members met with David Walker, the minister of public works, in November 1960. Harlow reported that "the Delegation had been well received. The Minister seemed to have been well briefed. He said that the National Library Building was still in the ten-year plan – meaning that it is supposed to be finished by 1966 ... He said he would take it up right away with the Prime Minister and the Cabinet and ... would let the Association know. He then asked if Mr. Harlow would send him a summary of the data and comments presented today."[15] However, the estimates for 1961-62 again included no provision for a National Library building. The CLA executive continued to bombard members of cabinet and the House of Commons and Senate with letters. At the recommendation of the past president, Bertha Bassam, two questions were added to the program of inquiry:

In what way does the National Library assist your type of library service?
In what way has your particular type of service been handicapped by the slow development of the National Library?[16]

The answers focused on three areas: the national union catalogue, the publication of *Canadiana*, and the references services of the National Library. A special general session on the National Library was held during the annual conference in St Andrews in 1961. Dr Lamb addressed the conference, and during discussion that followed, members of the association "brought to the attention of the National Librarian and placed on record some of the responsibilities that the library profession in Canada was expecting the National Library to assume, and facets of the role it would ultimately have to fulfil."[17]

Just days before the conference, the minister of public works had announced that funds for the building would be sought in the next fiscal year. But in 1962 it was reported that the government's austerity program might mean an indefinite postponement. A letter from the annual conference that year was forwarded to the prime minister. "On behalf of all Canadians, we earnestly implore that the construction of the National Library Building be not delayed and that it be retained as the top priority on any revised list of proposed building construction."[18] In reply, the prime minister informed the association that "no final decision has been made as to what public works projects will be postponed."[19] In late 1962, tenders were called for the erection of a building, and the following May a contract was awarded to Ellis-Don Limited of London, Ontario, for a building to be constructed by June 1966. This National Library campaign of CLA's second decade ended with the laying of the cornerstone by Governor General Georges Vanier on 10 May 1965.

In the years 1956-65 the *Canadian Index* and the microfilming project continued to grow. Both benefited from the establishment of the Canada Council in 1957. Over the next five years, the *Index* received funding to increase its coverage and to edit the twelve-year cumulation (1948-59), published in 1962. Though the number of titles indexed had increased to seventy-two by 1960, the *Canadian Index* was still limited to general-interest magazines. The other types of periodicals originally planned for coverage in separate parts of the index were never added, and the goal of "a national index for the approximately one thousand periodicals published in Canada which contain articles of reference importance" remained a dream.[20] The project still struggled with staff and financial shortages. Part-time employees frequently contributed more than their quota of work to ensure that monthly issues came out on schedule. The *Index* lost its three senior editors – Dorothy Chatwin, Margaret Wodehouse, and Ruth Mulholland – in 1955-56. (Both Wodehouse and Mulholland would return to the *Index* later.) They were succeeded by Julia Cockshutt as editor and Isabel Lee (later Bradley) as associate editor. Lee became editor for a short time beginning in June 1957.

A system of pasting up entries, which could then be photographed and reduced, was introduced in 1960 and resulted in a neater, more compact publication. An experiment was made in 1962 with machine indexing, but in these early days, too many adjustments were required to accommodate the index to what was described as the "prima donna aspect of some of the machines."[21] Until a larger, full-time staff could be employed, more mechanization would have to wait. The twelve-year cumulation was a major undertaking for the association. The total cost was $75,000, of which the Canada Council grant amounted to less than a third. When *Canadiana* took over the listing of films in 1964, the index became the *Canadian Periodical Index*, the name by which it is best known.

Eleven periodicals were added, bringing the total to eighty-three, of which twenty were in French. The cumulation of the *Index*'s predecessor and namesake for the years 1938-47 appeared in three fat volumes in 1966.

Subscribers had increased to approximately 400 by 1960 (they would reach 835 only seven years later). A subscription secretary, Beryl Steele, was appointed in 1962, and she actively pursued every potential buyer. More libraries and larger budgets in the 1960s also contributed to the increase in the number of subscribers. A raise in rates at the end of 1964 was accepted by most subscribers. The following year a new method of setting rates was introduced. The total cost of indexing any one periodical would be shared among the subscribers to that title. With the increase in subscribers, the financial position of the *Index* stabilized. The National Library continued to assist by paying the printing bill for the annual cumulation. In early 1965 the *Index* was the only project with a debt, and the $4,000 borrowed from the Elizabeth Dafoe Bursary Fund was expected to be repaid by the end of August.

The microfilming project received several grants-in-aid from the Canada Council between 1958 and 1962 directed at undertakings that were "beyond the project's pay-as-you-go limitation": long runs of newspapers, scattered files requiring extensive research, and newspapers from New Brunswick, Newfoundland, Prince Edward Island, and the Eastern Townships of Quebec, whose sales were likely to be small.[22] The filming of several long-running newspapers, such as the *Halifax Gazette* for 1752-1800 and the *Montreal Gazette* for 1785-1867, was completed. A grant of $12,000 from the Centennial Commission in 1964 enabled the project to fill gaps in the Confederation period, 1862-73. *Fate, Hope and Editorials*, a catalogue of over one hundred newspapers from this era, with excerpts from their editorials on issues of the day, was compiled by Helen Elliot of the microfilm staff and published as a centennial project. The microfilm camera had been moved out of the Public Archives building in 1965 to an air-conditioned office on Metcalfe Street, just around the corner from the main office. The rent of the new quarters would be recovered by the saving in staff time and transportation with this more convenient location.

The Canada Council also provided scholarships for research, including some sponsored by CLA, such as John R. Baird's doctoral thesis on Canadian provincial libraries, later published by the association. Elizabeth Morton found herself writing letters on behalf of applicants and advising them on how to prepare their applications. About Beatrice Clement, she told the Canada Council: "I have been particularly interested in Miss Clement's work because I feel very strongly that we should encourage the writing of children's works in bilingual editions ... The lack of a common reading background for our English language and French language boys and girls ... is a real hindrance in the sharing of books by the children of two language groups when they meet and as they grow up."[23] She advised Violet Coughlin of the McGill Library School, "Your paragraphs regarding the importance of adult education work I thought were very helpful, but I would try to prepare a factual outline of exactly how you plan to attack your Ph.D. ... I think the more factual your application is the better it will be received."[24] Sometimes Morton was forced to be more creative. She told Barbara Dawson of the University of Saskatchewan Library, "Unfortunately your copy paper had become pretty badly clouded so I had to use my imagination as to just what you had said. However, I think it will be all right."[25] By the standards of the 1990s, some of the details Morton provided in her letters of recommendation seem unduly personal, but they show her keen interest in everyone she helped.

A new project, Canadian Library Week, was inaugurated in 1959 at the recommendation of the committee on library-publisher relations. CLA was one of the sponsors of the program, which was set up as a private corporation based in Ontario. A poster and a bookmark were designed and a newsletter and leaflets produced to promote the project. Publicity was sent to magazines, bookstores, and radio and television stations. The CLA office supplied some staff under contract, but the project nevertheless stretched its limited resources. In June 1961 Elizabeth Morton urged Council that planning for the 1962 week go forward immediately over the summer. The previous fall, work had been "needlessly heavy" because little had been done in advance. Between 1963 and 1967 the Canadian Library Week issued *Canadian Library Horizons*, an annotated index to annual reports and other library publications compiled by Sophia Preisman. By 1967 financial support for the week was "far too little for the task," and attempts to raise more money "brought nothing or very little." "A great burden has fallen on a few persons each year – persons who have given hundreds of hours outside of their own regular job time in order to produce what has seemed to be for the most part a meaningful and certainly worthwhile project."[26] After much discussion, it was decided, with regret, to discontinue the project, and the corporation was wound up.

With the launching of *Feliciter* in January 1956 to carry reports and working papers for workshops and conferences, tentative programs, book lists, news notes, and ephemeral material, the CLA *Bulletin* could concentrate on general interest articles and the occasional issue devoted to special topics. It also carried articles by authors outside the library profession, including one by Walter de la Mare on poetry and another by C.S. Lewis about "Three Ways of Writing for Children." Longer and more scholarly articles were relegated to the occasional papers. After some issues in which the "Canadian Library" part of the *Bulletin*'s name had been printed in larger type, the Council in 1960 voted to change the name to simply *Canadian Library.* A catalogue of the association's publications that appeared in the January 1965 issue ran to twenty-two pages, including the index. The series of occasional papers now numbered sixty-two.

The Association at Twenty

At the end of its second decade, CLA had ten sections. The new ones formed between 1955 and 1965 were adult services (1955, originally called circulation services), the Canadian Music Library Association (1956), the Canadian School Library Association (1961), and the Canadian Association of College and University Libraries (which split off from the research section in 1963). The cataloguing section was now called technical services. The reference section would soon be renamed information services, and the research section, research and special libraries. A number of the sections published their own newsletters, some with imaginative names, such as the Canadian School Library Association's *Moccasin Telegraph.*

Following the 1957 conference in Victoria, the Council considered a petition for a public libraries section. Councillors were concerned that such a section would cut across the work of all the existing sections, except perhaps research. There was a lengthy discussion about the effect of having sections by type of library as well as type of activity. When CLA had been established, its organizers had tried to avoid repeating in the Canadian organization "the 'crazy quilt' situation of ALA."[27] A committee established to review the section organization of CLA presented an interim report the following year. It addressed the problem of fragmentation and overlapping: "Most of the members are interested in nearly everything – this is as it should be but it complicates section organization."[28] Although it had been association policy to form only sections by type of activity, several type-of-library sections already existed. The committee recommended that the number of signatures required to form a section be increased to fifty, that a prospective section serve a probationary period of at least three years as a committee, and that it justify its existence by a "continuous significant programme in its field of interest."[29] An equilibrium had to be maintained between the interests of the sections and those of the association as a whole. "The agreed-upon division of responsibility between CLA and its sections," Elizabeth Morton later wrote, "is that while the purposes of the association often can best be served by the association acting as a corporation through decisions and resolutions by its annual general meeting, the Council, and the board of directors, there are particular interests of certain types of libraries and certain types of library service that call for the grouping of like members into sections."[30] Instead of a new section, the interests of public libraries were brought together in a new committee, with subcommittees devoted to standards, salaries and working conditions, and statistics.[31]

Budget restrictions introduced earlier would be continued for the 1965-66 year. CLA might still, as John Archer said in 1963, be "trying to run a $100,000 Association on a $45,000 budget."[32] But at the end of its second decade, the association's financial situation was stronger. The deficit would soon be eliminated, and money borrowed from capital funds repaid. An increase to the fee scale had been introduced in 1964-65, and although there were some drop-outs, membership increased over the year to 2,542, more than three times what it had been at the end of CLA's first year. The activities of the association were under review by a special committee, which sent out a questionnaire to the membership in the fall of 1965. Great change and the almost unthinkable retirement of Elizabeth Morton were on the horizon, but the association celebrated its twentieth annual conference in Toronto stronger than it had ever been.

With the increasing membership came more work for the executive office. Renewal notices had to be sent out (a second one was mailed in October if members had not responded to the first in August), and records kept up to date on Addressograph plates. Individual clipping files were also maintained for all members. When the directory was revised for the January 1965 issue of the *Canadian Library*, nearly 50 per cent of it required changes: members were moving across the country, new libraries had been opened and new positions created, and there had been numerous retirements.

On the head office staff, too, fell the task of coordinating the increasing number of sections and committees so as to avoid duplication. In 1963 the committee on committees had reminded the chairs of sections and committees of their responsibility to keep the executive office informed about their activities, "as several of the sections now have sub-committees whose interests are very close to separate committees of the Association."[33] Like presidents before and after him, Neal Harlow had paid tribute to "our headquarters staff and our indefatigable Secretary" and to "the devoted and intelligent service that has been rendered to us, a service frequently beyond the call of duty ... If overwork is a criterion of pioneering, then our headquarters staff are pioneers of a caliber that should make us, their employers, highly uncomfortable."[34]

Early in 1965, in anticipation of her retirement three years later, Elizabeth Morton described her duties as follows:

1 Secretary to the Council and to the Board of Directors
2 Editor-in-chief of all publications passing through the office
3 Editor of *Canadian Library*
4 Editor of *Feliciter*
5 Office manager for the Executive Office
6 Publishing manager for all publications produced by the Executive Office
7 Executive Director of the Association in all matters of policy, working in the closest co-operation with the Board of Directors and the Council
8 Director of the Clearing House Services of the Association
9 Administrative Secretary of the Microfilm Project
10 Financial consultant of the Canadian Index Project
11 Co-ordinator of the conference programme and arrangements, many of which have to be made several years in advance, and prior to the election of the President of the conference year
12 Co-ordinator and consultant of the committees and sections of the Association
13 Librarian of the Association's library of professional literature
14 Representative for the Association at conferences, particularly those held in Ottawa of associations and government departments which co-operate with the Association
15 Liaison officer with Federal government departments from whom libraries wish concessions or redress
16 Consultant to individuals who wish to join the library profession, or who are anxious to change their jobs without advertising the fact, or wish to come to Canada and are uncertain about their credentials.[35]

Not mentioned in this list are the field trips Morton continued to make, though with the increasing demands on the association, travel funds were severely limited. In 1959 she travelled to New Brunswick to discuss the microfilming of that province's newspapers with the heads of libraries and other institutions. The year

1961-62 saw her visiting the Eastern Townships, Manitoba (in connection with an upcoming conference and as guest of the Manitoba Library Association), and Saskatchewan (at the expense of the province). The following year, visits to Saskatchewan and Minneapolis were paid for by the groups she addressed. In November 1963 the transportation costs for a trip to British Columbia and Alberta were borne by the University of British Columbia Library School, since Morton was to be a visiting lecturer for a week. In 1964-65 she gave a series of lectures to the master class at the McGill Library School and spoke to the Tennessee Library Association.

From time to time, business and pleasure took her overseas. A trip to Britain and the continent in 1961 included meetings of the Library Association in London and IFLA in Munich. Two years later Morton attended the IFLA conference in Sofia, Bulgaria, and visited Italy and Greece. This excursion was combined with a holiday so that it "did not carry any transportation costs to the association."[36] She described it as "the dream of a lifetime."[37] Her account reveals both the joys and the hazards of travel.

> Several of my Grecian adventures were completely unplanned such as losing one of my suitcases between London and Athens and having to do without its contents for 10 days. I felt a little like the Swiss Family Robinsons as I took a census of what clothes remained and how little I need buy in Athens in order to be suitably clothed for my seven day trip on the Stella Maris as it journeyed through the Greek Islands to Istanbul and back to Piraeus. My worst loss was the various eye drops which I was still using following the eye infection which I contracted while in Winnipeg. However, with dark glasses and an umbrella and the inevitable salted water, I managed.
>
> As a student at Dalhousie I had the good fortune to take my archaeology under Dr. James Falconer who was not only a lover of art and an outstanding Classics scholar but also well versed in the history of the New Testament. This meant that I had a good background to enjoy the past glories of Crete, Rhodes, Ephesus, Istanbul, Delos and Mykonos ...
>
> On my return to Athens my bag was still missing but fortunately it turned up that evening on the plane from London.[38]

A highlight of this trip was a visit to the Vatican Library, where she saw medieval manuscripts being microfilmed in colour, and cleaned and mended in the "library hospital."

During these trips someone else had to take over the administration of the office, sometimes giving up other duties to do so. Proposals were made repeatedly over the years that a full-time assistant or secretary for Elizabeth Morton should be hired, but the association's financial situation and the low salaries it could offer always prevented the filling of such a position. At a Council meeting in October 1963, the past president, Ruby Wallace, described the lack of an assistant as "a very serious situation ... some means must be found to remedy the situation ... it could not be postponed indefinitely."[39] The problem would be brought up again and again at Council meetings, but it remained unresolved, though some assistance was provided for Morton with the creation in 1964 and 1965 of the positions of secretary and office manager.

As secretary to the Council and board of directors, Morton provided essential continuity, explaining why things were done the way they were and furnishing the history of projects and other factual details. Her letters to members of Council had been a regular feature since the establishment of the association, but in 1964 they were cancelled "in the interest of economy." A year later she wrote, "I think that this was a false economy as it led to the Council not being as closely in touch with the work of the headquarters office as it should be. I am therefore reinstating the Council letters and you should receive monthly reports from now on."[40] For those who served on Council, Morton was always "cheerful, ready to give or seek advice, tolerant, and very circumspect in speaking to or about the shortcomings of others. Nothing wishy-washy, always firm and controlled, always headed politely toward what she saw as the welfare of CLA. She was a loving mother to all the members, ready to guide them gently out of their errors."[41] Dean Halliwell recalls her "sweet half-smile as she gently but ever so firmly put the straying sheep of CLA Council back on their destined track, whose every mile was clear in her mind."[42] Many who knew her commented on her ability to judge people. Kaye Lamb recalls how she was frequently able to place the "right person in the right place at the right time."[43] Bruce Peel once met her on the street during a conference. He "witnessed her dismay when she heard who had been appointed chair of a committee. She indicated that the person was a non-achiever. She dropped the committee from the CLA roster, and the committee was never heard of again."[44]

Her long experience and her understanding of human psychology are evident in the advice she gave to organizers of the Toronto conference in 1965:

Never fly low in obtaining a speaker. The best speaker will frequently come to your meeting if he or she feels that your meeting is of importance. It is up to you to show him not only that the meeting is important, but that he plan to make it of such importance to your group that out of it will come the necessary action and policy to further the terms of reference of your section. There is no need to put up with a secondary speaker if you can get a first rate one by exercising a little ingenuity, imagination, and know-how yourself.[45]

As editor of *Feliciter* and *Canadian Library*, Morton could work quickly and arrive at the essence of a problem. Some evidence of her methods remains in the association's files. In May 1963, for example, she took a two-page press release from the American Library Association about a new book journal and with a few swift strokes of a pencil gave it a title, cut or reworded sentences, and produced a more concise entry for *Feliciter*.[46]

A profile of Elizabeth Homer Morton appeared in the American publication *Current Biography* in 1961. In addition to describing her career, the article provided more personal details about the executive secretary, then in her late fifties, and incidently revealed a clue to her effectiveness as a manager. "Elizabeth Homer Morton has blue-gray eyes and gray hair, weighs about 145 pounds, and is five feet and one-half inch tall. She is a Presbyterian and an independent in politics. Modest about her own achievement, she once wrote that she does not save newspaper clippings about herself because she 'belongs to the Waste Paper Basket School of Thought.' In her leisure she listens to music and enjoys the company of cats. A bibliophile, she is interested in examples of fine printing and especially admires Eric Gill, whose Four Gospels is her most prized possession."[47]

Morton saw the many difficulties faced by the CLA office as a challenge. In her annual report, she described 1963-64 as "a year of fantastic problems guaranteed to arouse all one's ability towards the finding of imaginative and sensible solutions."[48] As Doris E. Lewis remarked at a Council meeting in 1964, "the staff obviously gave full value which was reflected in the amount of work done by the Executive Office on a limited budget."[49] New equipment was often badly needed. When Ruby Wallace asked Morton one day, "Elizabeth, what would you do if someone left you $1,000?" she replied, "Well, Ruby, I would be delirious with joy because I hope that the Directors would immediately spend it on equipment."[50] A bequest of $1,000 did indeed come to the association from Wallace's estate in 1965, to be used as the directors deemed best. Morton listed the equipment the office needed:

1 a Selector addressograph driven by electricity to replace one driven by hand – $500

2 a tape recorder for reporting conference speeches, meetings, etc., which will play back at a dictation speed – $200
3 for the telephone, an intercom system with three incoming lines – $100
4 a Xerox 911, "which will save our staff from having to make addressograph mats from articles and from copy sent in well typed" – $100
5 more shelving for the library – $100 [51]

By October 1958 the executive office had moved from 46 Elgin Street to a historic building, Hope Chambers at 63 Sparks Street, built in 1910 for the booksellers James Hope and Sons. (The building retains the inscription "Bible House" on the pediment.) The consolidated quarters "greatly added to the effectiveness of the work and welfare of the staff. Space for small meetings is now available."[52] Though there were still a large number of part-time and casual employees, a shift had been made in the late 1950s to fewer part-time and more full-time appointments.

Dean Halliwell recalls the CLA office in those days as a "homey" place. The staff "were very much a family – at least in the way they appeared to a visitor ... equally dedicated, approachable, and helpful."[53] In May 1965, just before the annual conference, the staff described "A Day in the Life of the CLA – ACB Executive Office" for an article in *Canadian Library.* This account was intended to "bring to life some of the excitement, interest, satisfactions and frustrations with which [the office] copes daily."[54] As each staff member arrives, she (or he – the great majority are women) is introduced to the reader, who is told about her background, her family, hobbies, and interests, and her duties at CLA. There were now thirty-eight employees, of whom nineteen worked part time. By 8:00 a.m. several members of staff have arrived, and the offices are opened and the staff worksheets prepared. Elizabeth Morton arrives at 8:30, hangs up her coat, confers with several members of staff, and then goes to her office to read her mail, dictate her replies, and "deal with reports until her appointments begin."[55] By 9:30 the office is "humming with activity. Its three telephone lines are constantly ringing with both local and long distance calls. Miss Morton's appointments begin with a call from Mrs. Doull, Research Staff, Royal Commission on Bilingualism and Biculturalism" (455). Her lunch is combined with a committee meeting on Canadian Library Week. Some staff working a half day leave at 1:00 and others arrive. Isabel Bradley, who has two small children, works on the *Index* at home. In the afternoon, Morton consults with staff on equipment, conference plans, and a draft of the public library standards.

Charlotte Whitton phones for information to answer a query on her radio program. Meanwhile, on the floor below and at the Public Archives, microfilm staff are checking material to be filmed and working out schedules. The senior camera operator, Roland Guttadauria, will arrive at 11:00 p.m. and work through the night.

After most of the staff have gone home at the end of the afternoon, Elizabeth Morton "has an opportunity to work uninterruptedly at the Dictaphone and then to editing and checking proof for *Canadian Library*. At 5:15 the night staff start to arrive and Morton takes a dinner break of one hour" (459). Staff who come to work after 5 include the multilith operator, those responsible for collating, stitching, addressing, and mailing publications such as *Feliciter*, Betty Crosby Faurschou, who is editing the 1938-47 cumulation of the *Canadian Periodical Index*, and Margaret Duncan, who does the filing. "Since the office has space limitations the quiet evening hours provide the opportunity, for example, to work on the clearing house files to collect information for questions which have come in the mail or over the phone, to organize new undertakings and to prepare for the days ahead so that all dead-lines may be kept" (460). By 10:30 all but a few staff will have left the office, "pulling the heaviest front door in Ottawa shut behind them."

5

CLA in an Age of Change, 1965-71

William Castell's acceptance speech on assuming the presidency of the Canadian Library Association in 1965 disturbed many members. In its November issue, *Feliciter* published a disclaimer that the new president had "queried many Association policies and procedures *from the personal point of view.*"[1] The agenda for the Council meeting at the end of October focused on the issues that Castell had raised. Members of Council were assigned specific topics and asked to be prepared to speak to them. Council reviewed the "position of the president and the president-elect as regards personal freedom of speech at an Association meeting,"[2] and at Castell's suggestion, a vote of confidence was taken in his presidency.

What issues had he raised in his speech that so challenged the organization? He questioned its nature and purpose and its committee structure. He expressed concern about the calibre of library education. He proposed that the profession take the use of "sub-professionals" seriously and stop "looking down our noses" at their training as if it was "a sort of 'back-door' ingress into libraries."[3] Finally, he raised the issue of bilingualism in Canada and within the profession.

With regard to CLA, Castell revived an idea that had been first raised in the 1950s. "I wonder ...," he speculated,

> if the association should become, or indeed, could it ever become, a professional association in the same sense that the Canadian Bar, Canadian Dental, Canadian Medical associations are? or should it remain what it is apparently now "all things to all men, or at least many things to many men" ...
>
> At one time this association had spawned no less than 73 committees – to say nothing of sub-committees. And like Old Mother Hubbard sometimes the cupboard was very bare. I raise this question because last year at Halifax I was a little appalled when

I heard the treasurer submit the financial report of this association. And not a single member, myself included, raised a voice in protest. Instead we raised the fees.

But I do think that after 20 years it is fit and proper that we examine again the role that this association is playing, or should play, in the lives of professional librarians in the country.

... There is no question in my mind but that some of the programmes and projects of the association have ... lured its members to live beyond their means, and it is the intention of your Board of Directors to implement a policy not so much of retrenchment, but rather a policy of "pay-as-you-go." It is our intention to place this association on a sound financial footing and to be wary of programmes and projects that are likely to become financial liabilities.[4]

The agenda for the October Council meeting pointed to the examples of the Library Association in Britain, which "a few years ago took the momentous step of changing from a general library association to a professional librarian's association," and the American Library Association, which had remained "a general library association."[5] With the development of professional groups at the provincial level in Canada, it had been suggested that the regional associations assume the role of professional organizations, "leaving general library association work to CLA." Strongly differing opinions were expressed by councillors. One felt that CLA "could achieve nothing by becoming a professional association,"[6] another that the organization should be moving in that direction. There was a lengthy discussion of the role the association might play in the life of the professional librarian: giving the individual a sense of belonging to a profession, overcoming provincialism, providing intellectual stimulation through work with others, and improving working conditions.

When the time came to discuss the correspondence received from members regarding Castell's speech, which "varied from commendation to humiliation, outrage, etc., etc.,"[7] Elizabeth Morton provided some historical background. The association's founders had been determined to avoid the situation of ALA at the time. The president there "was controlled heavily by the executive."[8] The president of CLA, it was felt, should be free to be a leader, and the presidential speech was therefore never vetted in advance. Other presidents before Castell had given speeches that had aroused controversy. On this issue, John Archer remarked, "If we say to the president 'you say what you wish,' then we can hardly condemn him for having spoken."[9] At the same time, the Council agreed that members have the right "to speak back as had been done, and that right is also a tradition of the Association."[10] The Council took two votes: one of confidence in Castell and the other reaffirming the "traditional powers and privileges of the president."[11]

CLA and Bilingualism

More provocative than Castell's comments on the nature of CLA had been his views on bilingualism.

> It is .. my considered opinion that Canada is, and will remain, a predominantly English speaking country. That is just a fact of life ... And any suggestion that a second language in Canada could ever attain equal parity with English, either by legislation or any form of political blackmail, is just wishful thinking ...
>
> There is no denial of equality or partnership on the part of English speaking Canada, and there never has been.
>
> Nor should French speaking Canadians nurse any sense of inequality or inferiority ... Let there be less emphasis on special privileges and more on friendly co-operation.[12]

Behind these remarks lay the Halifax conference of 1964, at which the first general session had been devoted to a discussion of libraries and Canadian dualism. The speakers had included Edmond Desrochers, the outgoing president, and Claude Ryan, then managing editor of *Le Devoir*. Desrochers had proposed the theme the year before. When he assumed the presidency in June 1963, he too had given an acceptance speech that many members considered provocative. He had pointed to the fact that at the founding conference in 1946, the association had undertaken

> to establish itself on the very foundation of the country it wished to serve, with its duality of languages and cultures ...
>
> We know that real bilingualism in Canada shall be the duty and prerogative of a minority of a cultural élite ...
>
> The French speaking members, for the common good of the association's annual conference, expect that nearly all lectures and discussions be held in the English language, as in the past, and the theme proposed does not imply even any indirect desire or request that the conference become bilingual ... So the bilingual character of the annual conference is not the object of the present examination of our association. It is Canadian dualism. If we are realists, we know that if some progress is to be made in that direction

from now to the 1967 centennial and well beyond, that progress is essentially bound up with the capacity of Canadian libraries and Canadian librarians to foster, to promote, in some measure, this Canadian dualism ...

... A new dimension is needed to bring our country to its continuation towards progress: a greater mutual awareness of the two cultures; a greater mutual understanding, on the basis of sharing in some measure of the two cultures.[13]

Desrochers pointed to some examples of the way that French had been neglected in even the most basic functions of the association:

The constitution of the association itself in its present revision only exists in English, although earlier editions were in both English and French, thanks to the kindness of Mr. Jean-Jacques Lefebvre, Dr. Raymond Tanghe, Mr. Claude Aubry and other French speaking members of the Constitution Committee. I only ask a question: is this the wish of the members of the association? ... When our Council decided to give an English title with a French and English sub-title to our bilingual Bulletin, this was generally accepted, except by Mlle Hélène Grenier, and as you may suspect, except by a few other French speaking members of this association.[14]

Though CLA had official liaison with a number of provincial, regional, and local library associations in the country, it had no affiliation with the Association Canadienne des Bibliothécaires de Langue Française. The decision not to pursue a Canadian accreditation program, which would be up for review in 1965, had had a negative impact on the unaccredited library schools of French-speaking Canada. Desrochers challenged the association to reappraise its activities in light of Canadian dualism. "C'est là, tout simplement, semble-t-il, se conformer aux exigeances mêmes du caractère bilingue de cette association créé pour répondre aux besoins de la dualité canadienne."[15]

Elizabeth Morton later reported, "After Father Desrochers' speech in Winnipeg we had members wishing to leave the Association ... After the Halifax conference there were more protests – this time there were some French as well as English protests. In fact some of our French members were bitterly hurt by certain sentences in Father Desrochers' speech, as they felt that they had suffered intensely to be members in a predominantly English-speaking library association and that Father Desrochers had not given them credit for this."[16]

The Association Canadienne des Bibliothécaires de Langue Française (ACBLF) had been founded as the Association Catholique des Bibliothèques d'Institutions in 1943. It did not become "a broadly based association of francophone librarians and libraries until 1948."[17] With a new focus and a new constitution, the ACBLF grew rapidly, from 150 members in 1948 to 459 just three years later. Significantly, francophone membership in CLA in the same period dropped from 206 to 169. Though some librarians from Quebec maintained membership in both organizations, most did not. In 1953 Claude Aubry proposed a French section in CLA, but no action was taken. When the program of inquiry was established in 1960, the ACBLF was not invited to contribute, even though, as Father Desrochers pointed out, its members were in a better position to survey library needs in Quebec than the largely anglophone Quebec Library Association. Indeed, it was the only library organization that could reach four-fifths of the libraries in the province.[18]

Despite the decision in 1946 that CLA should be a bilingual organization, the realities were very different, as Desrochers had observed. Distinguished francophone librarians had served on Council and the executive, but the minutes of these bodies reveal that French was never used. Not until 1949 was there a session in French at the annual conference. The *Bulletin* and its successor, *Canadian Library*, only occasionally published articles in that language. Even such basic publications as *Standards of Service for Public Libraries* did not appear in French until a year or more after the English version. Though Joseph-Antoine Brunet had been second vice-president in 1946-47, it was not be until 1963 that the association had a francophone president, and Desrochers would prove to be the only one in its history. The absence of French in CLA's activities can, of course, be attributed in part to lack of money, but it is not surprising that francophone librarians felt more at home in the ACBLF.

Desrochers succeeded in establishing a liaison committee between CLA and the ACBLF, which met for the first time during the Halifax conference in 1964. It discussed issues of common interest, including the brief to the Royal Commission on Bilingualism and Biculturalism, the accreditation of library schools, and the indexing of Canadian periodicals. However, for the Council meeting that reviewed Castell's speech a year later, bilingualism and CLA's relationship with the ACBLF were not on the agenda. It would appear that the issue was not yet taken seriously by most members. John H. Archer, who followed Castell as president in 1966, was more committed to improving relations between the two groups, but when the liaison committee met in June that year, no agenda had been prepared and the committee's future was in question.

Frustration within the ACBLF was mounting. At its August 1966 convention, the francophone association passed a lengthy resolution calling on CLA to consider becoming officially an English-speaking organization, leaving the ACBLF to represent francophones nationally. Only then, the ACBLF suggested, could a profitable dialogue be established. CLA was asked to make a decision "within the year." The October Council meeting agreed to establish a joint CLA-ACBLF committee, but no such group seems to have been formed. However, the inter-library association liaison committee, meeting in Winnipeg in March 1967, prepared a series of proposals it called the "Winnipeg Memorandum." It urged the CLA Council to "make provision in a revised constitutional structure for representation on its governing body of ACBLF and each provincial and professional library association" and to "sponsor jointly with ACBLF the formation of a co-ordinating Council representing CLA/ACB, ACBLF and the provincial and professional library associations."[19] An officer of CLA should be assigned to "close liaison among provincial and national organizations."

In June the ACBLF informed CLA that unless some action was taken, the francophone organization would sever its ties with CLA. When no reply had been received from CLA by August, the ACBLF passed a resolution at its annual conference suspending all relations. It fell to the new CLA president, Amy M. Hutcheson, to meet this challenge. She had the idea of establishing a "dialogue committee" with representatives from each organization. The group met on 22 October and passed a resolution recognizing "two national associations": CLA to be the English-speaking organization and the ACBLF the French-speaking one. The ACBLF approved this statement in November, and it was accepted by the CLA Council in March 1968. Hutcheson, in the meantime, had written to the 160 personal and institutional francophone members of CLA to ask if they thought that CLA should declare itself an anglophone organization and whether such a move would affect their membership. A majority of the eighty-five who replied were in favour of the change.

The proposal that CLA become a unilingual organization was presented to the membership in the form of an article in the May issue of *Feliciter*. "An Introduction to the Association Canadienne des Bibliothécaires de Langue Française: Its History, Role, and Relationship to the Canadian Library Association" was written by Basil Stuart-Stubbs of the University of British Columbia Library, who had been among the councillors most strongly in favour of the change. A resolution to recognize the role of the ACBLF in representing francophone interests nationally and to acknowledge the essentially anglophone character of CLA was passed "without significant opposition" at the 1968 conference at Jasper. In

Stuart-Stubbs's view, it was a sign "that English-Canadian librarians had belatedly confronted the reality of the Canadian situation as it affected their organization."[20] During the summer of 1969 members were informed that as of 1 September, the official name would be simply the Canadian Library Association.

Amy Hutcheson later commented, "It seemed such a good beginning for a real bilingual approach instead of a pretend version."[21] But after a few cooperative ventures in the late 1960s and early 1970s – such as joint briefs on the National Library and exchange visits between anglophone and francophone regions of the country – CLA and the ACBLF (which in the 1970s became the Association pour l'Avancement des Sciences et des Techniques de la Documentation) went their own ways. The hope that each community might participate in the other organization was not fulfilled. A few francophones continued to be members of CLA, but as Stuart-Stubbs commented in 1977, "English-Canadians have not increased their participation in ACBLF."[22] National organizations, not surprisingly, reflect the larger issues of the countries in which they evolve. Stuart-Stubbs remarked pessimistically in 1994, "One can see the C.L.A.-A.C.B.L.F. divorce as a microcosmic version of what seems to be pending for us as a nation. Unfortunately, I think this will have the same result: two solitudes."[23]

Other CLA members have expressed regret, but also a feeling that "the split was inevitable."[24] John Archer comments, "I didn't believe that the French side really wanted CLA to be more French – they wanted, rather, a separate organization that might later join CLA in some loose association."[25] Dean Halliwell's feeling, "then as now, was that it was only natural that francophone librarians should have their own organization, in which they could feel comfortable and could address their unique concerns."[26] Marion Wilson agrees that CLA made the right decision.

> With the best will in the world it was impossible for CLA to operate as a completely bilingual association in the first 25 years of its existence ... The principle obstacle ... was lack of money. To have attempted complete bilingualism would have jeopardized the already shaky financing of ongoing projects. The temper of the times in Quebec in 1967 led to dissatisfaction with the token bilingualism of CLA. I, for one, was pleased with the decision to abandon CLA's very inadequate efforts to serve both anglophone and francophone numbers.[27]

June E. Munro feels that Elizabeth Morton had "worked hard to make francophones feel welcome" in CLA.[28] But Stuart-Stubbs believes that she did not fully understand the issue. He points to her account of the association in the *hommage* presented to Father Desrochers in 1977, in which "she glosses over the matter as a mere change in name."[29]

A Study of Canadian Libraries

The annual conference in 1966 had passed a resolution that drew attention to the lack of adequate library service in many parts of Canada and called on CLA to "proceed immediately to define the terms of reference for a Canada-wide study of all aspects of library service, finance and related matters, and that it seek funds with which to conduct such a survey."[30] The Canadian library resources survey committee was established in October. At the same meeting of Council, the Canadian Library Research and Development Council (CLRDC) presented a proposal for a study to be completed in twelve months at a cost of $75,000. The Canadian Library Research Foundation, as it was originally called, had been created by CLA in 1957 at the suggestion of the scholarships and bursaries committee

(a) to provide bursaries, scholarships and fellowships in the field of library education;
(b) to provide grants in aid of, and to undertake research in library problems and services;
(c) to receive and administer grants, gifts, bequests, devises and endowments for the above purposes.[31]

The foundation was inactive in the first few years, but in June 1960 it held its first annual meeting and a board of directors was appointed. Two years later it hired a firm of consultants to advise it on the practicality of a major fund-raising campaign for a lengthy list of research projects. The consultants' report pointed to the many obstacles that would face the foundation. "The public does not realize that librarianship has emerged from 'a polite occupation' and is increasingly becoming a profession; that today's librarian is not merely a curator of books, but an important director of information."[32] "Business men (and others) are inclined to regard libraries as the responsibility of governments; national, provincial and municipal."[33] The foundation would be in strong competition for funds with "the requirements of health, hospitals, universities and social services, which are given far higher priorities in the public's estimation."[34] Because the consultants felt that "foundation" was misleading, the body's name was changed in 1964 to the Canadian Library Research and Development Council. When the study of Canadian libraries was proposed at the 1966 conference, the CLRDC saw it as the "major research project of national significance" that could, if successful, enable the CLRDC to make a more general appeal for funds.[35]

The library resources survey committee presented an interim report to Council in March 1967. It proposed a steering committee of twelve persons, who would select a director and a team of researchers for the project. The committee felt that eighteen months and $195,000 would be required. Six paid surveyors would have to be hired. A steering committee, chaired by Katharine L. Ball, approached Dr Lowell A. Martin, who was then at Grolier Incorporated in New York. His advice had already been sought by the association in connection with public library standards, and his studies of library service were widely known. After meeting with the committee in October, Martin submitted a provisional budget for a two-year study. The projected cost had now risen to $373,000. At his suggestion, the scope of the study was extended beyond a survey of existing conditions to the potential influence that libraries could have on users and non-users across the country. Public hearings would be held, and there would be special studies of urban, rural, northern, and multilingual areas. The information gathered was to be "a springboard for the real objective of the Study – the formulation of a national library plan for the future."[36]

But where was the money to come from? This was the greatest problem facing the survey, and it would prove insurmountable. The steering committee had chosen not to invite the CLRDC to participate, despite Ball's view that "unless CLRDC is involved in this project it might as well fold its tent and disappear."[37] Although he had been connected with the CLRDC since its inception, John Archer felt that this was not a good enough reason for turning over to it the fund-raising for the survey. He also feared that the CLRDC would not be content with a fund-raising role and the steering committee might lose control of the project.[38] A special assessment of CLA members was considered, but rejected because it was known that some members thought the fees were already too high. Instead, the 1967 annual conference expressed its "interest and support for the immediate implementation of this project" by proposing that individual and corporate members of the association contribute voluntarily toward the preliminary planning and fund-raising.[39] A donation of one dollar was suggested for individuals and from two to ten dollars for institutions, depending on their size.

Over the next months, the steering committee struggled with the problem of funding. An informal approach was made to the Carnegie Corporation of New York in December 1967, but CLA was informed that the Commonwealth fund was fully committed to projects in Africa and the West Indies. The Council on Library Resources stated that the survey was not within its scope, and the Ford Foundation also turned CLA down. Ball reported to the committee, "Frankly, your Chairman thinks that the American foundations feel that Canada should be able to support its own research and that any financial aid going outside the United States should be directed at the poor nations."[40] Appeals to Canadian foundations and agencies were equally unsuccessful. In June 1968 the steering committee recommended to the board of directors that the study be dropped.

The board decided instead to investigate the possibility of a more limited survey. Bruce Peel was asked to carry out this investigation. Early in 1969 he submitted a report that made two suggestions: existing surveys of libraries should be examined "with a view to extracting significant data," to be consolidated into a single report, and a survey should be undertaken of the "contribution good library service could make in changing the social outlook of people dwelling in a rural pocket of poverty with a view to contributing to the solution of the problems of the area."[41] The objective would be to obtain the support of governments for improved library service in the poorer areas of the country. These proposals were approved in principle, and the financial implications were to be examined.

In the meantime, there remained the problem of what to do about the pledges of financial support that had already been received for the larger study. A personal letter was sent to each donor asking if he or she would honour any pledge to the extent of expenditures already incurred. Whether the feasibility of the much-reduced study was ever pursued is unclear, but by 1969 the project had been abandoned, another victim of CLA's perennial inability to raise money for major undertakings.

Centennial Year: On View to the World

In 1967, the centennial of Canadian confederation, the annual conference was held in Ottawa. The highlight of the conference for many members was the official opening by Prime Minister Lester B. Pearson of the National Library – Public Archives building, to which all conference delegates were invited. Elizabeth Morton had had the opportunity to view the building early in 1966. As she described it in a letter to Council in March that year, a select party consisting of herself, Erik J. Spicer, and Guy Sylvestre had been taken through the building by Kaye Lamb and the dominion archivist. "We were all greatly impressed by the building, and by the excellent planning which has gone into its layout. I trod on air for several days afterwards because of the delight in seeing this dream for Canadian library service coming through in the form of so magnificent a structure."[42] Many CLA members, too, saw the National Library as the association's greatest accomplishment and the opening of the building in 1967 as the Canadian library profession's finest hour.

In celebration of the opening and Dr Lamb's imminent retirement, CLA commissioned a portrait of the national librarian from artist Lawren P. Harris. Money for this portrait was donated by "the Canadian library community and some Americans – trustees, librarians, publishers, library boards, friends of libraries, friends of Dr. Lamb, to mark the high regard in which he is held personally and to celebrate the official opening of the National Library – the high-water mark of his accomplishments for archives and libraries in Canada."[43] Individuals donated one dollar each, and institutions from one to ten dollars.

The association also marked centennial year with several awards: to the Centennial Commission in recognition of "the outstanding encouragement and financial support" it had given "to libraries, authors, and publishers in order to imaginatively and enduringly commemorate 100 years of Confederation"; to *Quill and Quire*, "which for over thirty years has consistently encouraged and supported an interest in books, libraries, publishing and the men and women responsible for these in Canada"; and to the University of Toronto Press and Les Presses de l'Université Laval for J. Russell Harper's *Painting in Canada: A History/L'Histoire de la peinture canadienne*, "a volume outstanding in format, beautiful as to illustrations in colour and in black and white, representative of all Canada over a long period, wide in its range of interests and written in both English and French."[44]

Another undertaking for Canadians in 1967 was to host the general council of the International Federation of Library Associations (IFLA), held over ten days in August. Librarians from this country had probably been attending IFLA conferences since the organization was founded in 1927. Now it was their turn to organize this international gathering. A general secretariat was established at the CLA headquarters in Ottawa, with Elizabeth Morton serving as coordinator and Margaret Wodehouse as secretary. Committees for local arrangements were chaired by Robert Blackburn in Toronto, Erik Spicer in Ottawa, Blanche Faucher (of the ACBLF) in Montreal, and Pierre Matte in Quebec City. The conference itself was based at Victoria College in the University of Toronto, and the plenary sessions were held in the concert hall of the Faculty of Music's new Edward Johnson building.

Three hundred and twelve delegates representing twenty-six countries attended. Simultaneous translation was provided in English, French, German, and Russian. Plenary sessions were open to observers, as well as the fifty Canadian delegates allowed under IFLA rules. "This was the first introduction of many Canadian librarians to the 'jet set' of librarianship ... For the uninitiated, the conference was an overwhelming whirl of great names ... The great mingled easily with the neophytes. Recent graduates bandied words with the authors of books and articles they had studied."[45] Particularly successful was the International Festival of Stories held by the children's section of IFLA at the Central Library Theatre of the Toronto Public Library.

Delegates made excursions to Niagara Falls and the Stratford Festival, where they saw a production of Gogol's *The Government Inspector*. Following the conference, they could visit the newly opened National Library in Ottawa, the Library of Parliament, and other libraries and public institutions. In Montreal they had an opportunity to see Expo 67, as well as the Bibliothèque Nationale du Québec and the libraries of the Université de Montréal and McGill. Those who went on to Quebec City had breakfast in Trois-Rivières (they had had to rise at 5:45 that morning), toured the Université Laval, strolled along the Promenade des Gouverneurs, and attended a banquet given by the Quebec government. After these tours of Canadian cities, delegates moved on to Boston, Washington, or New York.

The Canadiana library in the Canadian pavilion at Expo 67 had been assembled by Elizabeth Morton under contract with the federal government (she had prepared a similar library for the World's Fair at Brussels in 1958). It was "a working library on Canada connected by Telex with some fifty libraries across Canada in the interests of reference and information."[46] The collection included books, periodicals, and microfilm produced in recent years in the two major languages, English and French, together with examples of Canadian writing in some thirty other languages. Visitors were encouraged to browse, view microfilm on the reader, and ask questions, which might be sent by Telex to one of the connected libraries.

Remaking the Organization

In 1963, CLA had established an activities committee to review the current program of the association and make recommendations for the future. In the fall of 1965 a questionnaire was sent to all CLA members requesting comments and suggestions. In reporting to the annual general meeting the following year, the committee observed of the original activities report in 1946, "So comprehensive was that programme that it occupied the Association for twenty years."[47] In the meantime, the profession had "developed in numbers, strength and purpose. The 1966 Report of the Activities Committee reflects the comments and criticisms of an active association, the experience of a score of years, the aspirations of a maturing profession."[48] The committee noted two "significant movements" in responses to its questionnaire:

> One is an appeal for more involvement of younger members in the activities of the Association; the second is a cry for an emphasis on the professional aspects of librarianship ... The criticisms ranged from protests over high membership fees, through claims that the Association is dominated by the public libraries, and in the hands of a clique, to statements that there is a lack of communication but too much paper, to the despairing charge that no one in high places in Canada pays any attention to the CLA – ACB in any event. The praise saw CLA – ACB responsible in the main for higher standards of pay, of service and of support; for much accomplished in so short a time; for solid achievements through the "Canadian Periodical Index" and the Microfilm Project, for firm stands on tenure issues, to a general "well done" for the work of the Executive Office and headquarters staff.[49]

Among the recommendations of the activities committee were a strengthening of headquarters staff to allow the executive director more time for field visits and to enable the association to respond appropriately to public issues; the establishment of an accreditation procedure for Canadian library schools; and a review of the publishing program, the *Canadian Periodical Index*, and the microfilm project. "The response from membership," the committee observed, "brought to light a deep underlying concern with the future of the Association. The effectiveness of the present constitution was questioned. The matter of professionalism of the Association and within the Association was raised. The constitution of the Executive, the Council and the Sections was queried. Stemming from this concern were a number of critical comments on the need for more leadership, better communication, more professional inspiration from the national body. It was suggested that CLA – ACB should plan now to build its own home."[50] The report concluded, "The matter of the future constitution of the Association rests with the members and provision for full discussion should be made right early."[51] A president's advisory committee, chaired by the president-elect, was established to suggest ways to implement the recommendations of the activities committee. Nevertheless, change came slowly.

Margaret S. Gill, chair of the Canadian Library Council, under whose direction preliminary investigation was carried on for the establishment of the Canadian Library Association

Freda F. Waldon, the first president of the Canadian Library Association 1946-47

Dr W. Kaye Lamb, president of the Canadian Library Association 1947-48

Elizabeth Dafoe, president of the Canadian Library Association 1948-49

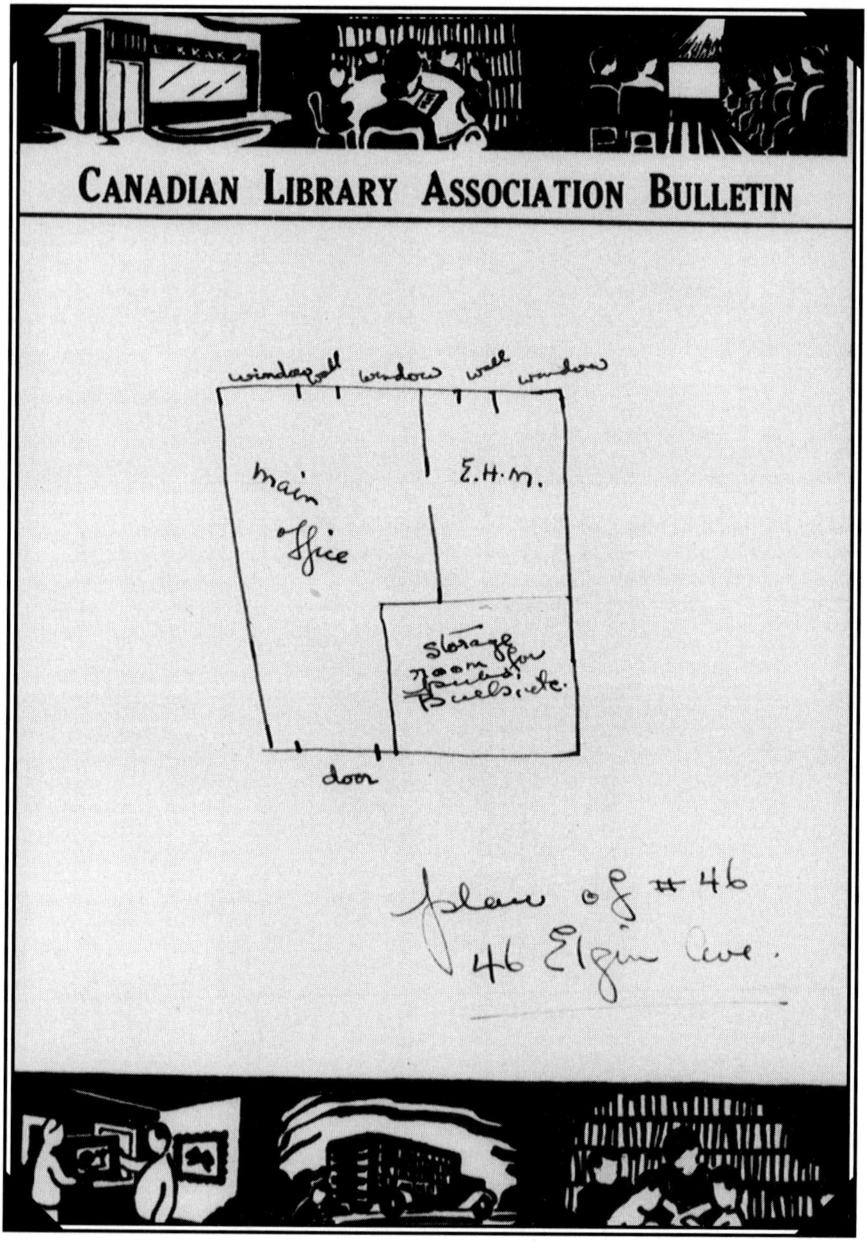

Elizabeth Morton's sketch of CLA headquarters at 46 Elgin Avenue, Ottawa (NA, CLA, 91-1)

Attendees at the fifth annual conference, Montreal, 9-15 June 1950. Back row includes Auguste-M. Morisset and Mayor Houde. Front row includes Elizabeth Dafoe, Kathleen Jenkins, Elizabeth Morton, and William Stewart Wallace

Kathleen Ruby Jenkins, president of the Canadian Library Association 1949-50

Marion Gilroy, president of the Canadian Library Association 1951-52

Edgar Stewart Robinson, president of the Canadian Library Association 1952-53

Peter Grossman, president of the Canadian Library Association 1953-54

Margaret Clay, Donald Crowdis, President Anne Hume, and Peter Grossman at the closing luncheon of the 1954 (Halifax) conference

A view of the central office, 1955: Mary Byrne (filing) and Doreen Mackay. Note the collating bins, Addressograph files, and library clearing-house files

Anne Isobel Hume, president of the Canadian Library Association 1954-55

Willard Ernest Ireland, president of the Canadian Library Association 1955-56

Mary Elizabeth Donaldson, president of the Canadian Library Association 1956-57

Bertha Bassam, president of the Canadian Library Association 1959-60

CLA headquarters staff, 1955. Seated (left to right): Dorothy Chatwin, Elizabeth Morton. Standing (left to right): Margaret Wodehouse, Julia Cockshutt

Ruth Scott working on the mobile membership wheel in the central office, 1955

The public library boards of Niagara Falls and Stamford receive at the 1956 (Niagara Falls) conference. Left to right: R. Urquhart, William Graff, Gladys Thompson, Willard E. Ireland, Eileen Weber, and George King

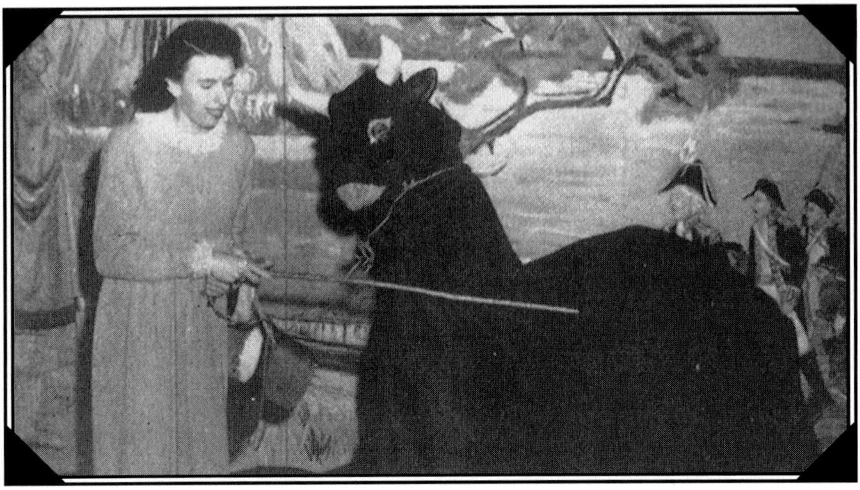

Laura Secord (Dorothy Van Slyke) and her cow (Helen Lothian and Edith Albrant) at the 1956 (Niagara Falls) conference

Neal Harlow, president of the Canadian Library Association 1960-61

Three presidents of the CLA-ACB: Rev. Edmond Desrochers, SJ (1963-64), Ruby Wallace (1962-63), and Robert Hamilton (1961-62)

Left to right: Gerard Moisan, Alberta Letts, Robert H. Blackburn, Dr Jean Bruchési, and Dr W. Kaye Lamb at the 1958 conference, Quebec City

David Foley, president of the Canadian Library Association 1964-65

John Hall Archer, president of the Canadian Library Association 1966-67

Amy Margaret Hutcheson, president of the Canadian Library Association 1967-68

Katharine Lucy Ball, president of the Canadian Library Association 1968-69

Alita Vikse, Bruce Peel, Roberta Wilson (Weiner), and June Munro at the 1959 (Edmonton) conference

Marion C. Wilson, field and executive secretary of the Canadian Library Association 1967-70

Elizabeth and Mollie Morton

W. Kaye Lamb and Governor General Georges Vanier laying the cornerstone of the National Library and Public Archives building

The official opening of the National Library, 20 June 1967, Prime Minister Lester B. Pearson at the rostrum

Margaret Wodehouse and Ruth Mulholland, editors of the Canadian Index to Periodicals and Documentary Films, 1948-49, *with the boxes containing the 200,000 cards on which the copy of the 12-year cumulation went to press*

Bruce Braden Peel, president of the Canadian Library Association 1969-70

Martha Shepard, president of the Canadian Library Association 1970-71

Dean Wright Halliwell, president of the Canadian Library Association 1971-72

Publications. A committee, chaired by Brian Land, dean of the Faculty of Library Science at the University of Toronto, was formed in 1968 "to consider the overall publishing policy of the Canadian Library Association, with reference to the quality and content, financing, printing and sales of periodicals and other publications."[52] In a report presented to Council the following March, the committee recommended that the principal CLA publication, now called the *Canadian Library Journal*, should be "a prestige publication rigidly edited."[53] It should carry articles that made "a contribution to the overall philosophy of librarianship." *Feliciter* should be discontinued (it has, in fact, continued in various formats to this day, and it is the *Canadian Library Journal* that has ceased publication), and a new newsletter, designed so as to be more attractive but still reasonably cheap, should be issued nine to ten times a year. It should carry general news and information for the association. The committee further recommended that newsletters published by the sections recover their costs within the fiscal year through fees. New methods of producing and cumulating the *Canadian Periodical Index* should be investigated. Miscellaneous publications should be carefully scrutinized for their sales potential. Commercial firms should be used for the association's printing unless material was urgently needed or only small quantities required. The publications policy committee also proposed that it be reconstituted as an editorial and publications policy committee to oversee the association's publications. An editor-in-chief and director of publications should be appointed as soon as financially possible. The committee warned that the continuing financial stability of the association depended on an "effective and profitable publishing program."[54]

These major recommendations were endorsed by the board of directors and the Council. In reporting to Council in November 1970, the new editorial and publications policy committee made a number of recommendations for ensuring the effectiveness of any publications, "whether to be sold or distributed free of charge, proposed by Sections, Committees, Workshops or other groups within the Canadian Library Association."[55] There was considerable discussion as to whether the new procedures impinged on the rights of sections, and some recommendations in the report were redrafted or withdrawn. However, Council approved the principle that publications to appear under CLA imprint must be referred to the editorial committee for review. It also supported the proposal that a publications development fund be established, from which money could be drawn to launch new publications.

In May 1967 the *Canadian Library* had observed, "Undertakings which were dropped by CLA – ACB in the 1950's because of lack of interest and support by the membership at large are now being dusted off and discussed enthusiastically. Examples are professionalism and a code of ethics to be debated at the 1967 Conference."[56] At that conference John Marshall had presented a paper on "Chapter Status – Solution to Our Problems?" and F. Eugene Gattinger had spoken on "The Role of a National Library Organization in Canada." The incoming president, Amy Hutcheson, proposed that Council review, over the next year, the personnel and organization of the executive office, the constitutional organization of CLA, and its publications, conferences, programming, membership involvement, and fees. Relevant passages from the two papers given at the conference and from the report of the activities committee were provided as background. Council reviewed the Winnipeg Memorandum at the fall meeting, and it was proposed that affiliated provincial, regional, and professional library associations be invited to appoint one representative to an advisory group which would meet with CLA Council "on an experimental basis ... for a period of three years."[57] Members of the Council advisory group (CAG) attended Council meetings beginning in the spring of 1968 and also met as a separate body chaired by Aileen Tufts.

The Council Advisory Group. "Although it is not stated in the motion which brought it into being, the circumstances surrounding its creation dictated that the Council Advisory Group's primary task would be to draw up a plan for the restructuring of CLA."[58] The group's first report in the fall of 1968 made some radical suggestions. It proposed that the association be restructured as a federation. The officers of the association, in addition to the president and past president, would be four vice-presidents representing "four pillars" of CLA – the Canadian Association of College and University Libraries, the Canadian School Library Association, the Canadian Special Libraries Association (now the research and special libraries section), and a new Canadian Public Libraries Association[59] – and five regional representatives elected at large. The national organization would be structured on a biennial basis, with conferences every two years. Regional or local workshops and conferences would be held in the intervening years. There would be a minimum number of standing committees, and ad hoc committees would be dispersed as soon as their tasks had been completed. Projects would be undertaken by the federated organizations, each of which would also be expected to develop a first-class journal in its field. The CAG was asked to prepare a detailed structure for this hypothetical new organization in time for the June Council meeting.

Its feasibility study for a federation of library associations was presented to the membership at the annual conference in St John's in 1969. One member of the group, Albert W. Bowron of the Scarborough Public Library, presented what he called a "minority report" in the form of a resolution. It called for CLA to be disbanded, since in its twenty-year history it had "failed to improve significantly the stature of libraries and librarians, to influence governments to improve their support of libraries ..., to solve the many technical and organizational problems with which libraries have been faced." Further, the association did not "reflect the multicultural and bilingual nature of this country, is not representative of its regional nature and does not represent the native peoples of Canada."[60] In the view of one observer, "Bowron's revolutionary proposal and condemnations did not quite detonate the explosions we expected, though the hearts of one or two senior and founder members of CLA did begin to bleed through microphones around the hall."[61] Some members felt that Bowron's resolution was premature, given that the CAG proposal had still to be discussed. In the event, he was persuaded by a majority to withdraw it.

During the summer of 1969, the CLA membership was asked to comment on the feasibility study. The task of overseeing this review fell to the incoming president, Bruce Peel. In presenting excerpts from members' comments in the September-October issue of *Feliciter*, he commented wryly, "Two years ago, had the CLA Nominating Committee given me the slightest hint that restructuring of our Association would come up in 1969/70, I would have had the good sense to decline office."[62] The level of response had been disappointing. "Member participation and involvement is the cry of librarians," Peel observed. "And what has been the response of our 3400 members? A dozen and a half letters at most. O Apathy, thy synonym is librarian!"[63]

Comments tended on the whole to be negative. One member asked, "Why restructure?" The only answer this individual could find in the CAG report was that "'in this age of rapid change many of our institutions are being subjected to examination.' Surely this is not sufficient reason for doing something – merely because everyone else is doing it."[64] Another described the proposal as "a most unfortunate mixture of good intentions, wrong assessments, and illogical conclusions which could do great damage to library service in Canada" (6). A number of respondents felt that an emphasis on type of library would be "divisive" (5), have a "fragmenting effect on the profession," and "place barriers of communication between various kinds of librarians and various geographic areas" (3). One individual was "distressed that in the statement of Responsibilities of the proposed Federation, we lose what I consider to be my main reason for supporting a national association, i.e., promotion of librarianship per se at the national level" (12). A proposal in the CAG feasibility study to limit full participation in the association to "professional members" roused criticism; CLA should be open to all "who work and/or are interested in libraries and their function in our society" (4).

The proposed biennial structure, in one person's opinion, "might slow down the work of the organization by half, since committees and officers might tend to save their energies and their substantial reports and proposals for conference years" (7). The organization might "lose members, not gain them ...," said another respondent, because there would be "a smaller Council, and fewer conferences. There is also the reduced possibility of participation in Council meetings and decisions" (9). Someone else agreed: "The new Council would cease to represent some of the type-of-library and type-of-activity sections which are now active ... [The reorganization] would kill off six CLA sections" (10-1). The only result, this individual thought, would be "to rouse them to action" (11). The principles suggested for committees were those that had always guided the organization, and "there is no reason to think a federation would be wiser or richer" (8).

When the Council discussed the restructuring proposal in November, Bruce Peel recommended that no decisions be taken at that meeting. General issues should be reviewed. These were the principle of federation as it would affect CLA, other organizations, and librarianship; the financial implications of the proposed new structure; the number and identity of constituent associations; and the authority and executive powers of the Council and officers. In summing up the lengthy discussion, Peel concluded that although Council was not "sold" on the form of federation proposed, it recognized the need to change with the times, to forge a closer liaison with regional associations, and to engage and commit members in the national organization. Any decisions should await a review of the proposal at the next annual conference. In the meantime, the board was asked to prepare a working paper setting out the various suggestions for reorganization, and the executive director would study the constitutions of other national library associations. This review turned out to be "more arduous than anticipated,"[65] and at the March 1970 Council meeting, it was proposed that a structural committee be established to make a thorough study of the issues. The new committee was to bring in a report not later than the spring of 1971. The CAG's three-year term, due to expire in 1971, was extended another year.

The Hamilton Conference of 1970. At the 1970 conference in Hamilton, Steven A. Horn of Carleton University Library, seconded by Erik Spicer, librarian of Parliament, presented a resolution that an ad hoc committee of representatives from each section of CLA review the objectives of the association by June 1971. This committee would either recommend "feasible structures necessary to attain the objectives" of the association or "that no feasible solutions ... can in fact be established, and that the Canadian Library Association as presently organized be dissolved."[66] As Horn later remarked, this resolution "may just have been too controversial for a good many members of CLA ... Its appearance elicited considerable heated debate marked with acrimony to the extent that the *Globe and Mail* devoted considerable space to the motion and debate on it the following day."[67] The resolution was referred to the Council from the general session. It would not, in any case, have been binding because it contravened sections of the CLA constitution and by-laws on committees. However, as Horn pointed out, it was "representative of a frustration of some CLA members with the Association's policies and structures which sometimes characterized the 1970 Hamilton conference."[68] He drew attention to four other resolutions that "either explicitly or implicitly" revealed such dissatisfaction.

The Hamilton conference produced a flood of comment. Issues of the *Canadian Library Journal* and *Feliciter* over the next few months published Steven Horn's comments on his controversial resolution and a rejoinder by the president, Bruce Peel, an article on reorganization by David Skene-Melvin of the Lake Erie Regional Library System, further comments on the Hamilton conference by Donald A. Redmond, chief librarian of Queen's University, and a plea from P.K. Mutchler, head of the Thunder Bay Public Library, that CLA re-examine its goals. As one member of Council commented, "It may be uncomfortable but it is healthy."[69] Charles MacDonald summed up the conference for his colleagues at Simon Fraser University in inimitable style:

> Why do we do it? Twenty-five times now, a sizable gaggle of librarians has got together to discuss the concerns of their profession and their Association. Far and wide over our true north strong and free we have met ... this time in Hamilton which – perhaps because of a good local arrangements committee – seemed much nicer a place than had been feared.
>
> What can 800-plus librarians find to discuss over a rather crowded week? And is it worth the while? ...
>
> ... To the honour of previous executives at last year's Conference, the question of

C.L.A.'s inability to serve the needs of librarianship was faced and proposals for drastic restructuring were presented. Further progress was to be made this year, "Challenge of the Seventies" you know. How to face C of 70: let's try an all day, no-coffee-break session of SEVENTEEN SPEAKERS ... let's get 800 people into a hot room and listen to all this stuff. One guarantee – they won't recover till the 80's. It was no great surprise that the next day considerations for change dribbled down the drain ...

But again, is it worthwhile? I think so – maybe. With this abbreviated vision of woe this may seem strange. But though *business* has its ups and downs from year to year, one thing is constant. Amazingly enough, although they appear as witless as academics in large groups, individual contact with librarians can be, and often is, both useful and stimulating.[70]

One of the 1970 resolutions concerned access to sectional and committee deliberations. It was resolved by the conference "that future planning and scheduling of section and committee meetings be such as to provide more open access to all members of the Canadian Library Association."[71] Council, in reviewing this resolution after the conference, accepted the principle of openness, "except when matters of confidentiality are concerned."[72] The committee on committees was asked to define procedures for open meetings. On the Horn resolution regarding policy and structure, it was the consensus of Council that the structure was under "active and competent review." A committee was established to consider the aims and objectives of CLA. Half the members of this group were to be CLA members who had joined the organization in the previous two years.

The ad hoc committee on aims and objectives, chaired by Dean Halliwell of the University of Victoria Library, presented its report to Council in March 1971. It assigned the highest priority to communication with members. Matters considered by the association and its board, Council, and committees should be reported to members fully and promptly. Membership response must be encouraged, and channels for the expression of membership concerns be developed and maintained. "To foster this sense of awareness and involvement, the principle of 'openness' must be adopted within the Association and all its constituent agencies."[73] Objectives concerning librarians included the promotion of high standards of librarianship and personal conduct, the protection of rights, duties, and responsibilities of librarians, and the implementation of standards relating to working conditions. With regard to libraries, the objectives included the promotion of public knowledge and support, the advancement of library interests with the federal government, the development of standards of service, and the facilitation of cooperation among libraries. A fourth group of objectives addressed issues in Canadian society, training for library service, relations with other associations, and the promotion of research and publication in Canada. The report of the committee was accepted by Council in March 1971 and presented to the membership at the annual conference in Vancouver that year.[74]

A New Structure. The work of the structural committee had been delayed by the resignation of the first chair and another member, who both felt that they could not afford the time involved. A new ad hoc committee on structure, headed by Douglas N. McInnes of the University of British Columbia Library, was established in the spring of 1971. Its terms of reference were to study the new aims and objectives, the written and recorded submissions of sections and individuals regarding restructuring, and the organization of other library associations, and on the basis of these studies, to formulate specific recommendations regarding the future structure of the association.[75] It was to present an interim report at the fall Council meeting and a final report in the spring of 1972.

In the opinion of the McInnes committee, organization by type of library offered the greatest membership appeal. It proposed five divisions – the Canadian Association of College and University Libraries, the Canadian Association of Public Libraries, the Canadian Association of Special Libraries and Information Services, the Canadian School Library Association, and the Canadian Library Trustees' Association – whose presidents would sit on Council.[76] Presidents of the four type-of-library associations (but not the trustees' association) would also serve on the board, together with the president, first and second vice-presidents, treasurer, and executive director. To address type-of-activity interests, there would be standing committees; the two proposed were technical services and information services. No member of the ad hoc committee on structure had favoured a federation of regional organizations, but provincial and regional associations would be represented on Council by their presidents, if they were members of CLA. There would continue to be nine elected councillors (this number was later changed to six). Full membership would be available to anyone employed in a library (later modified to all "persons interested in the promotion of librarianship and library service"). The basic fee would include membership in one division. Conferences and the basic structure of CLA would continue to be annual.[77]

This plan for restructuring the association was send to members in December 1971 and, with some modifications, would be approved with "near unanimity" at the annual conference in June 1972.[78] The new structure was significant in that, among other things, it spelled the end of any vestige of a purely professional association: the trustees' association became a full constituent member of the association (though it was not represented on the board), and the general membership was open to all with an interest in libraries. It also restored the regional representation originally rejected by the association's founders in 1946 because, according to Elizabeth Morton, it was "not close enough to the rank and file."[79] In its report for the year 1971-72, the board of directors looked forward to the changes this restructuring would bring – "the third stage of a rocket which it is hoped will send the Association into a new orbit of usefulness to the profession in Canada."[80]

The late 1960s and early 1970s had been an era of change. Revolt had also been brewing in the American Library Association, as Dennis Thomison describes in a chapter entitled "Response to a Changing World" in his history of the American organization. This changing world included many young librarians who had come into the profession from universities also in a state of upheaval and who saw their organizations as equally hidebound and dominated by a few "old people." The changes made to CLA in the early 1970s reflect the new emphases on individualism and on specialization. Looking back on that era, Dean Halliwell comments, "I believe that the pressure for review of the goals and organization of CLA was part of the general ferment of the time. Like so many things, it came to Canada a little later than it did to the United States ... Fortunately, I think that less of the Canadian process was driven by the 'anti-establishment, anti-Vietnam War, flower-power' atmosphere which I observed as a fairly regular attendee at ALA Annual and Midwinter conferences in, say, 1968 to 1972. Also fortunately, in my opinion, CLA never went as far in its espousal of causes whose connection with librarianship was minimal at best."[81] Bruce Peel felt that "the age and increased size of the CLA as an organization was a factor in creating a demand for change. The membership was expanding and many of the new people joining were young persons recently out of library school."[82] In Basil Stuart-Stubbs's view, "one of the catalysts must have been the pace of growth in libraries during the sixties ... Also, during the sixties many new post-secondary teaching institutions were created, and libraries were started from nothing. Under the circumstances it was inevitable that C.L.A. would follow the model of A.L.A. in developing sections by type of library or library function. These allowed librarians with common interests to meet."[83]

6

"When Elizabeth Leaves"

Any discussion of reorganization within CLA in the 1960s naturally included the question of a replacement for Elizabeth Morton, who was due to retire in 1968. As early as 1963 she had drawn attention to the fact that her contract expired in five years and that she would need a secretary for the last two, in order to hand over to her successor "a smoothly running machine."[1] Financial constraints had continued to prohibit the hiring of an executive assistant for Morton, but in 1964 and 1965 two new office positions were created. To relieve her of routine administrative functions, the job of office manager was created, and bookkeeper Mary Whittendale was trained for this task. Rosalind Godfrey joined the staff as secretary to the executive director. The position of assistant was finally added to the head office establishment in 1966, but it was dropped almost immediately for lack of money.

The board of directors had discussed the question of a successor for Morton at a meeting in February 1965. She pointed out that current salaries at the CLA office were based on the 1959 scale and "would not attract a competent person."[2] It was decided that an exploratory committee, reporting to the board, should be appointed to review the duties of the executive director and look for suitable candidates. The final choice and negotiation of the salary would remain with the board. The committee, made up of Bertha Bassam, Edmond Desrochers, and John Archer, had a year to report. On 1 July it submitted an interim report on the duties and responsibilities for an individual who would initially be an associate director. However, no appointment had been made by 1 September 1966, the date originally proposed. The review of the association's program by the activities committee, the necessity of dividing up the duties of the executive director, and continuing financial restraints all contributed to the delay.

An advertisement for the position of executive director finally appeared in the November issue of *Canadian Library* that year. The appointment was now to begin on 1 September 1967 to provide "6 months of liaison with the present Executive Director" before the new appointee took office on 1 March 1968.[3] Qualifications for the position – in addition to university graduation, a professional library degree from an accredited school, and administrative ability and experience – were "knowledge of Canadian libraries" and a "suitable personality." "The position," applicants were informed, "provides challenge, scope and excitement."

No one who applied was considered experienced enough, but there were two candidates with potential. In June 1967 therefore, the board proposed "a very active president" with two executive vice-presidents: a controller responsible for the budget, membership, fund-raising, publications, and all activities "that cost money," and an administrator responsible for liaison with committees, sections, and the regional associations, for conference work, and for public relations.[4] As the treasurer, Hugh L. Smith, later explained, the board was "in a box ... We felt it was not fair to put someone into the position as it is at present – the strongest personality might blunder. This position has been built up by one strong personality over 20 years and it is impossible to duplicate Miss Morton."[5] E.L. (Les) Fowlie, then director of technical information for The Architects Collaborative Inc. in Cambridge, Massachusetts, but with experience at the University of Alberta Library and the library of the Association of Universities and Colleges of Canada, was proposed for the position of executive vice-president controller; and Marion C. Wilson, who had worked in the executive office since 1963, was the choice for executive vice-president administrator. Wilson would take over her duties as of 1 June 1967, and Elizabeth Morton would cover the controller's position until Fowlie became available the following May. It was felt that one or other of the candidates might "work themselves into" the position of executive director.

This proposal for a division of powers was strongly rejected by the membership at the annual general meeting the following week. Marion Wilson described the reaction as "an uproar ... There was a good deal of talk of two-headed monsters."[6] She therefore withdrew her acceptance of the appointment. When the Council met again two days later, the proposed executive structure was reworked into three positions: the post of executive director was reinstated; under that individual would be a field and executive secretary, responsible for liaison with sections and committees, public relations, and conference work, and a controller and chief of publications, whose duties would be as previously determined. The treasurer estimated that 3,800 members would be required to produce the revenue needed to support all three positions. Since the membership was currently only 3,000, the controller's position would be filled when the money was available. Until she retired, Elizabeth Morton would carry the duties of both her own position and that of controller and chief of publications. Wilson was appointed field and executive secretary as of 1 September, and the executive director's position would be readvertised with a revised description. Council was in the embarrassing situation of having to ask Fowlie to resign. He and Wilson would be free to reapply for the position of executive director, which would have to be filled before Morton's retirement, now postponed to the end of April 1968.

The revised plan was presented to the membership in the November issue of *Canadian Library*. Charts were included showing the responsibilities of the three positions, and Marion Wilson was introduced. A graduate of the University of Alberta and the School of Librarianship at the University of Washington, she had worked in libraries in Seattle, Montreal, and London, England. In Montreal she had served as a library trustee for nine years and had been instrumental in obtaining a branch library for the suburb of Notre Dame de Grâce. Since coming to the CLA office in 1963, she had been associate editor of the *Canadian Periodical Index*. In 1994 she described how Elizabeth Morton had interviewed her while preparing to leave on a trip and while staff were "popping in and out with papers for her to sign ... All the while Elizabeth calmly talked to me as though she had nothing on her mind but my concerns and all the time in the world to devote to them."[7] At the end of an hour and with the staff pleading that the taxi was at the door, Morton offered her a position. "Still talking we went down together in the elevator and she caught her taxi and, I guess, her plane. I was to learn that this was a typical Elizabethan departure."

The advertisement for the position of executive director that appeared in the November 1967 issue of *Canadian Library* included a more detailed description of the duties and mentioned that the director would be "supported by two high-level professional staff positions"[8] (in fact, one had still to be filled and no one would be appointed in the next three years). To the qualifications had been added – belatedly – "the ability to read French quickly and easily. (Preference will be given to a candidate who is completely bilingual)." "Knowledge of Canadian libraries" had been revised to "wide experience and personal knowledge of the Canadian library scene." The position now required "personal qualifications which will enable the Director to identify with librarians across Canada and encourage the growth and development of an Association which will fit the needs of tomorrow and to-day." Any reference to the "excitement" it offered had been deleted.

Both Wilson and Fowlie did apply, but by January, Fowlie had withdrawn his application. However, a new candidate was now being considered. Clifford William Herbert Currie had been born in Canada and had received his early education in Glencoe, in southwestern Ontario. He and his family subsequently moved to England, where he completed his schooling. He attended the University of London, Cambridge (where he studied law), the Harvard Law School, and the University of London School of Archives and Librarianship. Having worked in various public libraries in Britain, Currie was now librarian of the Imperial College of Science and Technology in London. He had held office in the Library Association, IFLA, the International Association of Technological University Libraries, and other organizations. Though British by training and professional experience, he "visits Canada annually, keeping in touch with Canadian library affairs."[9] Candidates were interviewed by the board during the February Council meetings. It was unanimously decided to offer the position to Currie. If he declined, Marion Wilson would be appointed. Currie accepted; between Elizabeth Morton's retirement on 30 April 1968 and his arrival on 1 September, Wilson would be acting executive director.

Meanwhile, plans were secretly under way for a farewell dinner to honour the outgoing executive director. As Wilson later recalled, "All was going along merrily when suddenly one day ... all hell broke loose. Some member, whose name I have forgotten, dropped into Elizabeth's office to tell her how sorry he was not to be able to attend the dinner and to wish her good luck! She burst into my office, eyes blazing, and tore a strip off me. How dare I plot behind her back? How dare I organize a completely illegal operation? etc. etc. She could really show her displeasure when she wished to. We used to say to each other 'Watch out, she's in her "Miss Morton" mood!' But this was the worst I had ever experienced. Fortunately I was not frightened and just laughed at her. 'Do you really think that you were going to be allowed to sneak away like a thief in the night?' I asked her."[10]

With the board, Morton was more restrained, but just as determined. She had written to both the president, Amy Hutcheson, and the past president, John Archer, early in 1968 stating that she did not wish any dinners. At an executive meeting on 17 February, she spoke at length on the subject.

Not only was she loath to go through the taxing business of attending this dinner, but she was very conscious of the fact that the Council members were against this type of demonstration ...

Eventually, assurance was given to Miss Morton by the Directors that the dinner would be kept small, that no one would be pressured to go, that no Councillor need feel any obligation to attend, and that the dinner would be devoted to a group which, in true honesty, wished to have a get-to-gether with her in March. With this assurance, Miss Morton agreed to attend the dinner on March 30th.[11]

The dinner was held at the Skyline Hotel in Ottawa. Two hundred and fifty friends and associates from as far away as Victoria, Churchill Falls, and New Jersey attended. As Marion Wilson remarked, "she was, I am sure, very touched by the sight of the some 250 members who had come to Ottawa ... at their own expense – this was her family, gathered to honour her."[12] At the head table were Madge Gill, who had proposed Elizabeth Morton as executive secretary for the Canadian Library Council back in 1944, ten of the past presidents of CLA, and the current board of directors. Each of the past presidents in turn paid tribute to Morton. Robert Blackburn summed up what she had meant for CLA in a short poem entitled "The Weaver":

The fabric is wide and it's tough,
And the pattern ingenious enough,
  The warp was provided
  By us who presided –
Elizabeth furnished the woof![13]

Bruce Peel announced that a collection of essays, *Librarianship in Canada, 1946-1967*, was to be published in her honour. Morton was presented with a cheque, "earmarked as a scholarship for her studies at the University of Chicago," and a book containing an illuminated title-page and the signatures of seven hundred friends and associates.[14]

Elizabeth Morton's career and the evolution of the Canadian Library Association had been inextricably linked. In Florence Murray's view, it was unlikely that CLA without Morton "would have survived the early years to become the strong organization that it is today."[15] And Robert Blackburn had observed in 1959 that her "wisdom and ingenuity have helped bring the ship safely through unknown waters and through some periods of short rations and uncertain weather."[16] Like

Blackburn, many could not "imagine our profession without the CLA – ACB and without Elizabeth at the centre of it."[17] "When Elizabeth leaves," Dean Halliwell had remarked in 1967, "we will never quite recover from it."[18]

Morton's hard work and dedication were legendary. In Freda Waldon's words, she "has always attempted more than is humanly possible."[19] She told Council in 1967, "I work 12-14 hours a day for at least three months of the year, every Sunday either at home or in the office, half a day on Saturdays. By doing this I can control the policy matters."[20] Her long experience gave her great authority in the running of the organization. Marion Wilson quoted her as saying of the board of directors, "'they always do what I tell them.' This might sound a bit dictatorial but I came to appreciate that she made many decisions on her own and they were accepted because of the deep trust she inspired in president after president, in board after board, and in the membership at large."[21] Basil Stuart-Stubbs, who did not know her as well, described her as "a model of propriety, always seemingly in control of herself," but behind the self-effacing façade he suspected "a determined person with well-honed skills in management and even manipulation of others, including a succession of presidents and executives."[22]

Did she perhaps exert too much control? In answer to this question, Wilson commented that "in the last couple of years before her retirement, there were some rumblings of discontent."[23] In John Archer's view, because she had "little sympathy for cries of rights – not undergirded with assumptions of responsibilities," she was "at odds with the 1960-70's members who rebelled against the slowness of gradual development."[24] At the 1967 conference, "some harsh things were said about Elizabeth & her regime – all this before anyone could stop them. Elizabeth was terribly distressed ... as a friend I yet must say I think Elizabeth kept such a firm control of committees & agencies that there was going to be change either at CLA or more locally. It is the old conundrum – when does a remarkable career begin to inhibit necessary change."[25] June Munro also believes that Morton's "long presence as executive director could have inhibited a review of the organization. In her quiet way she was in control, and attempted to be involved in all aspects of the organization – the sections and the committees. It was more than one person could direct and manage."[26] Dean Halliwell, on the other hand, does not feel that her "presence in CLA until 1968 had any inhibiting influence on CLA's self-review," though he acknowledges that some people saw her approach as "old-maidish."[27]

The degree of control that Morton exerted over the organization was balanced by a complete lack of "self-seeking ambition." Kaye Lamb remarked at the retirement dinner, "She has always carried out the intentions of the Directors whether or not she entirely agreed with them. She has been an immensely loyal as well as an efficient servant of the Association."[28] As Munro has observed, the "interests and abilities of members of CLA executives varied greatly from year to year, and often E.H.M. had to assume additional responsibilities. I recall one CLA treasurer who did not get involved with finances, E.H.M. would prepared a yearly statement, and he would read it to the membership at the A.G.M."[29] Of great importance in an administrator, in Bertha Bassam's view, was Morton's "ability to hold a tight line when it is necessary ... We would not be where we are today if she had not done it, because it is the Executive Director who is the one person with the power and opportunity to see that continuity is maintained throughout."[30]

And then there were her personal qualities. Archer observed that "Elizabeth has always 'kept her cool.' She has never at any time shown any pettiness or bitterness. Three things have stood out – her honesty, her frankness and her sense of responsibility. When I have asked her to be frank and candid on a matter of policy she had done me the credit of criticizing it as she saw it."[31] Many remember her as "both a councillor and a confidante" in personal matters.[32] Martha Shepard recalls that she was "ready to help anyone with a problem, listening quietly, asking intelligent questions and then offering helpful advice. With her knowledge of libraries all over the country and the personnel in each one, she was in a position to offer informed advice which I know helped a great many people."[33]

Her patience with the tiresome was also legendary. She kept her dislike of some individuals well hidden. Though "she did not suffer fools gladly," she dealt with them "with great patience and finesse."[34] Katharine Ball "could not find any record that, to prepare herself for this job, she had taken any course in the Department of External Affairs under Professor Mike Pearson," but Ball did not think "the political, diplomatic and financial expertise that has been at the disposal of CLA – ACB for so many years was learned in a library – even in Toronto!"[35] John Archer remembers that Morton "had a wide knowledge of the Canadian democratic system. She knew who were the power brokers and she had a sense of timing that made her forays into public life sensible and telling."[36]

Bruce Peel commented that "she was very shrewd at sizing up people."[37] Her skill with people was evident in her methods of administration, which Bertha Bassam described as "original and interesting, well worth following if one had the wisdom and finesse to use them."[38] The working environment she created at the headquarters office was particularly suited to the needs of women, many of them married with small children and unable to work traditional fixed hours. An "extraordinarily kind and patient boss,"[39] she collected around her a loyal and efficient staff, and her "enthusiasm and tireless devotion to CLA were infectious."[40]

In writing of CLA's first twenty years in the festschrift presented to Morton after her retirement, Freda Waldon concluded, "Probably no one person can ever again have the intimate knowledge of the whole library scene in Canada, or of the work of the Association, that Elizabeth Homer Morton has acquired over the years; possibly no one person will ever again accomplish the sheer volume of work that she has, or occupy quite the place she has made for herself not only with our own membership but also with government officials and workers in related fields right across the country. Her going inevitably marks the end of an era."[41]

New Orbits of Usefulness

Elizabeth Morton had not really retired, of course. In the spring and summer of 1968 she took an extended trip to Britain and Europe, visiting Iceland on the way back. It was partly a holiday – galleries, museums, festivals, tours, even the occasional library – and partly to research the background of her Morton grandparents for a project fondly called "John and Sarah." After her return to Ottawa in July, she and her sister moved to a new apartment on MacLaren Street, in a building where an office might be available when she needed one. She then set off for Chicago in late September.

At the Graduate Library School of the University of Chicago, Morton completed her dissertation on "Libraries in the Life of the Canadian Nation, 1931-1967" and in 1969 was awarded the master's degree for which she had begun studying while executive secretary of the Canadian Library Council in the 1940s. In 1969 she also received an honorary doctor of laws degree from the University of Alberta, on the occasion of the graduation of the first class in library science from that university. It was only one of a number of honours that came to her in these years. She had been the recipient of a Centennial Medal in 1967, and in the following year had been made a member of the Order of Canada. In November 1970 Sir George Williams University (now Concordia) awarded her the degree of doctor of letters *honoris causa*. In presenting Elizabeth Morton for the degree, the university librarian, Helen Howard, described her as

> a prime mover in the post-war expansion of improved library service in Canada ...
>
> Since 1946 many new libraries have been built in Canada, and Canadians have better access to books and instructional materials than ever before. This impetus for change has come largely from the Canadian Library Association, working with governments and interested groups. Perhaps more than anyone else, Miss Morton has been the powerhouse within it. Enthusiasm, wit, and dedication are her trademarks.[42]

At her retirement from CLA, Morton had announced her intention to establish a consultancy. She was appointed to the Office of Library Resources at the National Library of Canada in the fall of 1969. There she supervised the completion of the survey of research collections in Canadian libraries begun by Joan O'Rourke, edited the data, and wrote the first report. Following O'Rourke's illness and death in 1971, Morton served as acting head of the resources survey section for a period of six months. Another project was the coordination of "Canadian books abroad" – packages of five to ten books selected for libraries in other countries that were interested in expanding their Canadian holdings. Morton worked with a committee of librarians and with staff from the Classic Book Shop in Ottawa. One packet consisted of books for young readers, and those for adults were organized around such topics as fiction, art, and nature study. The undertaking was supported by funds donated by Canadian librarians.

In late September 1972 Elizabeth Morton began an assignment that took her back to her birthplace. The government of Trinidad and Tobago had requested from UNESCO the services of a consultant to carry out a survey of library services in the islands and draw up a plan for a national library system. For three months she travelled, observed, and held interviews and discussions with librarians, educators, and government officials. Her report, *Trinidad and Tobago: Development of Library Services*, was published by UNESCO in June 1974.

Morton continued to give lectures and write articles and reviews. In 1971 she was a guest speaker at the annual conference of the Quebec Library Association. Three years later she delivered the Alberta Letts Memorial Lecture at Dalhousie University, published as *Developing Public Libraries in Canada, 1535-1983*. She contributed histories of CLA to the *Encyclopedia of Library and Information Science* (1970) and to *Livre, bibliothèque et culture québécoise* (1977), a two-volume work published in honour of Father Edmond Desrochers.

For *Queen's Quarterly*, Morton reviewed the report of the Royal Commission on the Status of Women, together with Kathleen Archibald's study *Sex and the Public Service*, in an article entitled "Raising the Status of Canadian Women." Two parts of her planned history of libraries in Canada from the earliest days, an expansion of her dissertation, appeared in the *Library History Review*, and a historical survey of library cooperation in Canada in *Library Trends*. A Christmas letter sent to friends in 1975 described three ongoing projects: the history of Canadian libraries and reading, to be called "The Wine of Words"; an account of the Canadian Library Council, entitled "The Future Beckons"; and her edition of the letters of Sarah and John Morton.[43] All these projects remained unfinished when Elizabeth Homer Morton died on 6 July 1977 after a long illness.

Clifford Currie: A Break with the Past

While she was in England in the spring of 1968, Elizabeth Morton had lunched with Clifford Currie, the executive director designate. She has left no opinions on the man or the appointment, but one wishes it were possible to eavesdrop on that luncheon between the two directors, outgoing and incoming. It is hard to imagine two more different people: Elizabeth Morton, who had devoted her life to Canadian libraries and the CLA, and Clifford Currie, who seems in retrospect to resemble those international high-flyers that Canadians had encountered at the IFLA conference in 1967.

British by training and experience, Currie seems a strange choice to head a national organization in an era of heightened nationalism, despite his Canadian birth. Indeed, Dean Halliwell has remarked that he was "a surprising choice to direct CLA, no matter what criteria one applies."[44] He was introduced to the membership at the annual conference in Jasper in June 1968 and took up his duties that September. In the three years he held the position of executive director, Currie seems to have had little impact on CLA, except to move the executive office into more expensive quarters in January 1971, quarters which the association soon found it could not afford. His legal training was useful in a period of organizational change. He was able to point out in March 1971, for example, that CLA had not followed the correct procedure for amendments made to the constitution in 1967, and they had therefore not taken effect.[45] But he apparently had no plans for the organization beyond getting "rid of the granny image."[46] Several people have commented on his "less than impressive organizational and leadership skills," which were matched with a "lack of familiarity with Canadian libraries, librarianship and life."[47] Isabel Bradley recalls him as "an often absent director, who travelled a lot and had illusions of grandeur."[48] In Dean Halliwell's view, his tenure did result in a "necessary broadening of responsibility and delegation of duties,"[49] though those who worked with him at the CLA office would describe his regime differently.

Early in his tenure, Currie decided not to prepare written reports for Council unless specifically asked to do so, perhaps one reason that to the outside observer he now seems a shadowy figure. But there is no shortage of anecdotes about Clifford Currie's personal eccentricities. A number of people recall his resemblance to the actor Peter Sellers, even "his eagerness to be mistaken for" Sellers.[50] Indeed, an observer at the 1969 conference stated that Currie not only resembled Sellers, but had studied his methods. He read the formal notice of meeting "in true Sellers style, perfectly straight-faced – except for a slightly fanatical gleam in the eye! It *couldn't* have been done for any other reason than comic relief. At any rate, it broke the audience up."[51] His very first move on arriving at CLA, Marion Wilson recalls, "was to redecorate Elizabeth's office completely, in dark colours. The darkness was compounded by his keeping his new, dark, drapes closed at all times ... Truly, going into his office was like going into a mysterious den! Only one lamp burned on his desk."[52] He lived in an apartment hotel in downtown Ottawa, moving his clothes and other belongings into the office when he went out of town on business.

> Harmless eccentricities no doubt. He was, however, obsessed with image and with personal power. And he seemed to have no idea how to make the best use of staff. We were a very loyal and willing crew but in the end he alienated most of us ...
>
> ... He gave no guidance, he didn't consult with senior staff. We had no idea what he was up to. He took no new initiatives, unless you count those in the image department. The old collegial spirit was gone from the office.[53]

Wilson, the second in command, moved to the National Library at the beginning of 1970, and Margaret Wodehouse resigned shortly after.

Why had Clifford Currie been chosen? Wilson seems a more appropriate candidate, although she admits that she was ambivalent about the job. Amy Hutcheson, who was president in 1967-68, recollects that the Council was aware "a vocal portion of the membership was restive at this time, inferring that CLA's image needed to be updated and 'smartened.' These people seemed to feel that

Elizabeth had a 'make and mend' philosophy which was appropriate for the past but did not suit the future. Because of this it was decided that [it] would be unwise to take the easy approach of appointing a well-qualified member of the existing staff."[54] Erik Spicer has suggested that Currie's bilingualism and an increased emphasis on internationalism in the library profession were reasons for his selection.[55] Another factor was the shortage of candidates: only a few applications had been received, one – Bruce Peel recalls – "a young person just out of library school."[56] Hutcheson remembers that when Currie came for an interview, "he made a very good impression ... I feel impelled to add that, within a year *I* knew that we had made a mistake ... But one thing is certain – we really *did* provide a break with the past!"[57]

More serious than Currie's eccentricities, however, or even his lack of leadership, were discoveries about irregularities in the finances during his tenure. In March 1971 he informed the board that he wished to resign not later than 31 August that year. He had "said on his application and has consistently maintained that he believed his own limit of effective service must be three years."[58] In fact, according to Martha Shepard, who was president at the time, the board of directors had decided not to renew Currie's contract; the board's decision "was based on solid evidence."[59] Shepard wrote to him in July asking him to explain travel expenses for a trip to Australia and advances for his attendance at the ALA midwinter and CLA conferences. He was requested to surrender his charge card, since the office manager had been authorized not to pay any future bills charged by him. Currie replied evasively, choosing in justification "to show what I have taken from CLA in contrast to what, perfectly properly, I might have taken."[60] He had, he claimed, refused salary increases in his second and third year and had paid into CLA funds all his lecture fees "without contractual obligation"; he had saved CLA untold amounts in legal fees; his travel for the association had been "dirty, squalid and exhausting"; he had been "devoted to CLA and its interests." After a further attempt to obtain an accounting of the expenses, the board decided that there was no hope of recovering anything and CLA should "cut its losses." It says much about Elizabeth Morton's probity during her twenty-two years as executive director that safeguards had not been put in place for her successor.

Clifford Currie left Canada for Britain, where he became librarian of the Ashmolean at the University of Oxford in 1972. Six years later he was appointed librarian of the Earl Gregg Swem Library at the College of William and Mary in Williamsburg, Virginia. The appointment "split the library staff ... causing bitter feeling within the library and between librarians and faculty members."[61] Initially, the United States Department of Labor refused Currie a work permit because the college administration had "failed to demonstrate that they were unable to hire a qualified U.S. worker for the position."[62] However, the college appealed the ruling, and he was admitted under a special provision for "distinguished practitioners of the arts and sciences."[63] Clifford Currie died in February 1994.

In Retrospect

What had the Canadian Library Association achieved in its first twenty-five years? Mention has been made – *pace* Al Bowron – of the founding of the National Library of Canada, expansion in library service across the country, and improvement in the salaries, working conditions, and professional status of librarians. Perhaps more revealing are the observations of those whose careers go back to the early years of the organization. "Before CLA was organized," Bruce Peel has commented, "individual librarians worked largely in isolation. The CLA gave us a national perspective, and kept us up to date on new developments in librarianship."[64] Roberta Wilson Weiner has also stressed the isolation of Canadian libraries and librarians before the founding of CLA and the part Elizabeth Morton played in bringing them together. Basil Stuart-Stubbs feels that the association's most important contributions were conferences and publications. "Conferences ensured that we got out, met other people, visited other libraries and generally found out what was happening. Between conferences we had two publications that kept us abreast of developments."[65] He also draws attention to the association's function as a lobbyist – "some of the things we took for granted (such as the postal book rate) existed because of CLA's efforts" – its promotion of library education, and the assistance it provided for librarians in understanding the new information technology in the late 1950s and early 1960s.

John Archer, who graduated from the McGill Library School in 1949, believes that "CLA impacted on all librarians & every aspect of library science. It was the meeting place, the clearing-house for all ideas & it brought experience & professional training together in a viable professional organization."[66] His contemporary Dean Halliwell describes the major effect that CLA had on his career as "getting me involved in the politics of librarianship; membership on CLA committees, or those of CACUL after its founding, and subsequent service on their Councils and Executives, including terms as President of both, brought personal satisfaction in involvement in aspects of librarianship outside the day-to-day routines of my professional position ...; without association activities, I probably would have had a much less happy career."[67] The ad hoc committee on aims and objectives in 1971 had stressed the importance of communication between the association and its members. For those whose careers began in the 1940s, the Canadian Library Association's most important function has always been communication – between librarians everywhere in Canada.

Appendix One: Conferences of the Canadian Library Association, 1946-71

DATE	PLACE
1946	Hamilton
1947	Vancouver
1948	Ottawa
1949	Winnipeg
1950	Montreal
1951	Toronto
1952	Banff
1953	Ottawa
1954	Halifax
1955	Saskatoon
1956	Niagara Falls
1957	Victoria
1958	Quebec City
1959	Edmonton
1960	Montreal (joint CLA-ALA)
1961	St Andrews, N.B.
1962	Ottawa
1963	Winnipeg
1964	Halifax
1965	Toronto
1966	Calgary
1967	Ottawa
1968	Jasper
1969	St John's
1970	Hamilton
1971	Vancouver

Appendix Two: Presidents of the Canadian Library Association, 1946-71

1946-47	Freda Farrell Waldon
1947-48	William Kaye Lamb
1948-49	Elizabeth Dafoe
1949-50	Kathleen Ruby Jenkins
1950-51	William Stewart Wallace
1951-52	Marion Gilroy
1952-53	Edgar Stewart Robinson
1953-54	Peter Grossman
1954-55	Anne Isobel Hume
1955-56	Willard Ernest Ireland
1956-57	Mary Elizabeth Donaldson
1957-58	Alberta Letts
1958-59	Robert Harold Blackburn
1959-60	Bertha Bassam
1960-61	Neal R. Harlow
1961-62	Robert Morris Hamilton
1962-63	Ruby Evelyn Wallace
1963-64	Edmond Desrochers
1964-65	David William Foley
1965-66	William Rentoul Castell
1966-67	John Hall Archer
1967-68	Amy Margaret Hutcheson
1968-69	Katharine Lucy Ball
1969-70	Bruce Braden Peel
1970-71	Martha Shepard
1971-72	Dean Wright Halliwell

Notes

ABBREVIATIONS

AL	*American Libraries*
ALAB	American Library Association *Bulletin*
CL	*Canadian Library*
CLAB	Canadian Library Association *Bulletin*
CLCB	Canadian Library Council *Bulletin*
CLJ	*Canadian Library Journal*
LJ	*Library Journal*
MTRL	Metropolitan Toronto Reference Library
NA	National Archives of Canada
NLC	National Library of Canada
OLR	*Ontario Library Review*
TPL	Toronto Public Library

CHAPTER ONE

The title of this chapter has been taken from an account of the 1946 conference written by Angus Mowat and published in the *Ontario Library Review*. The *Concise Oxford Dictionary* defines "glory be!" in its colloquial usage as "an expression of surprise or delight." Both emotions may have been present in Mowat's mind when he wrote the article.

1 CLA, Annual Conference, *Proceedings*, 1946: 3.
2 Waldon, "The C.L.A. – The First Twenty Years," 24.

[3] "Library Associations of Canada 1900-1946," 272.
[4] Morton, "Canadian Library Association," 174.
[5] Waldon, "The C.L.A. – The First Twenty Years," 24.
[6] *The Ontario Library Association*, 117.
[7] Ibid.
[8] Welling, "Canadian Librarians Meet at the American Library Association," 12.
[9] "Canadian Library Association," *ALAB* 21 (Aug. 1927): 226.
[10] "By Way of Introduction."
[11] Donnelly, *The National Library of Canada*, 41.
[12] Commission of Enquiry, *Libraries in Canada*, 143.
[13] "Canadian Library Council Formed," 462.
[14] NA, CLA, 87-3, CLC, Beginnings, 1940-1943, M.S. Gill and E. Barr to ----, 20 Nov. 1940 (photocopy).
[15] NA, CLA, 91-8, CLC, Minutes, 1941-1944, Library Association of Ottawa, April 1941 (photocopy with additions).
[16] Gill, "C.L.C. to C.L.A.," 17.
[17] Information in this section has been taken principally from the following sources: NA, CLA, 91-3, CLC, Salaries and Staffing, curriculum vitae for E.H. Morton; NLC, Library Development Office, untitled biography of E.H. Morton; *Canadian Who's Who*, 1973-75; *Current Biography Yearbook, 1961*; John Morton, *John Morton of Trinidad*; Tremaine, "Elizabeth H. Morton." The historian and librarian Arthur Silver Morton (1870-1945), who was also born in Trinidad, was Elizabeth's uncle.
[18] Morton, "Books to Delight."
[19] NLC, Library Development Office, untitled biography of E.H. Morton.
[20] Bruce Peel, reminiscences, 1994.
[21] Hutcheson, "Elizabeth Homer Morton," 16.
[22] *The Development of the New Brunswick Legislative Library*, 29. Her report was published in the *Journals of the Legislative Assembly of the Province of New Brunswick* in 1931.
[23] In 1954, ten years after she had left the library, she wrote to C.R. Sanderson to draw his attention to a Doves Press Bible listed in a recent dealer's catalogue (see MTRL, TPL Papers, Box 46).
[24] Tremaine, "Elizabeth H. Morton," 314.
[25] Ibid., 314-5.
[26] NA, CLA, 91-13, CLC, Salaries and Staffing, E.S. Robinson to C.R. Sanderson, 2 Dec. 1941.
[27] Ibid., M.S. Gill to C.R. Sanderson, 24 Jan. 1944.
[28] Ibid., C.R. Sanderson to M.S. Gill, 27 Jan. 1944.

29 Ibid., E.H. Morton to M.S. Gill, 23 Feb. 1944.
30 Ibid., M.S. Gill to members of CLC, 26 Feb. 1944.
31 NA, CLA, 87-5, CLC Bulletin 1944-1947, 1975, E.H. Morton, "Canadian Library Council Bulletin" (typescript, c. 1975).
32 Ibid.
33 Ibid., J. Fred. Hockay [?], undated letter.
34 NA, CLA, 91-5, CLC, General Meeting by Invitation, draft letter.
35 NA, CLA, 91-8, CLC, Minutes, 1941-1944, Library Association of Ottawa, April 1941.
36 "Events of 1945-46."
37 Lomer, "Background of the Canadian L.A.," 1108.
38 Ibid., 1110.
39 Mowat, "Glory Be!" 237.
40 CLA, Annual Conference, *Proceedings*, 1946: 61.
41 Ibid., 62.
42 Ibid., 58.
43 Harry Campbell, reminiscences, 1994.
44 Bruce Peel, reminiscences, 1994.

CHAPTER TWO

1 NA, CLA, Vol. 1, Council and Board of Directors, 1946, Report of the Secretary to Executive and Council, 25 Sept. 1946.
2 "CLA – ACB at Work," 310.
3 Ibid.
4 NA, CLA, 91-1, CLC, Establishment of, 1943-1947, E.H. Morton to F.F. Waldon, March 1947.
5 Ibid.
6 NA, CLA, 9-1, Executive Director, Reports to Council, 1947-52, Report for March 1947.
7 NA, CLA, 9-1, Executive Director, Reports to Council, 1947-52, CLA – ACB Expenditures, 1 Sept. 1946-1 June 1947.
8 *CLAB* 7 (Nov. 1950): 92-3.
9 CLA, Annual Conference, *Proceedings*, 1947: 26.
10 *CLAB* 7 (Nov. 1950): 92.
11 Talman, "Twenty-two Years of the Microfilm Newspaper Project," 140.
12 These problems were reported at the council meeting of 19-20 June 1947 (see NA, CLA, Vol. 1, Council and Board of Directors, 1947). Robert M. Hamilton, in reporting on the project in the CLA *Bulletin* the following year, perhaps for

public relations reasons, stated that the work done at Microfilming Services "was of the best quality" (*CLAB* 4 [Feb. 1948]: 91). The project would later use the company to process the films.

13 Talman, "Twenty-two Years," 141. There is a copy in NA, CLA, Vol. 72, Microfilm Project Publications, pt. 2.

14 Ibid.

15 NA, CLA, Vol. 72, Microfilm Project Publications, pt. 2, *Catalogue* (1948), 3.

16 Mackenzie King's letter of acknowledgement was published in *CLAB* 5 (Sept. 1948): 89.

17 These are the years the catalogues appeared in the CLA *Bulletin*. The third catalogue was published as a separate in 1951 and the fourth in 1954.

18 Talman, "Twenty-two Years," 142.

19 Quoted in "CLA – ACB at Work," 330.

20 Joyce Rous Sowby, reminiscences, 1994.

21 Welling, "Canadian Librarians Meet at the American Library Association," 11.

22 Morton, "A Century of Periodical Indexing," 80.

23 "CLA – ACB at Work," 329.

24 Ibid.

25 Isabel Bradley, reminiscences, 1994.

26 NA, CLA, 87-5, CLC Bulletin 1944-1947, 1975, E.H. Morton, "Canadian Library Council Bulletin" (typescript, c. 1975).

27 Waldon, "The C.L.A. – The First Twenty Years," 32.

28 NA, CLA, 87-5, CLC Bulletin 1944-1947, 1975, F.F. Waldon to George Dunning, 21 Aug. 1947.

29 NA, CLA, 9-1, Executive Director, Reports to Council 1947-52, CLA – ACB Bulletin, 1 Sept. 1950-31 Aug. 1951.

30 *CLAB* 8 (Nov. 1951): 74.

31 Morton, "20 Years A-Growing," 292.

32 Waldon, "The C.L.A. – The First Twenty Years," 23.

33 NA, CLA, Vol. 1, Council and Board of Directors, 1947, Minutes, 23-24 Oct. 1947.

34 Foley, "The C.L.A. as Publisher," 39.

35 "CLA – ACB at Work," 314.

36 Quoted in Donnelly, *The National Library of Canada*, 43.

37 Canadian Library Association et al., "A National Library for Canada," 4.

38 CLA, Annual Conference, *Proceedings*, 1961: 99.

39 Canadian Library Association et al., "A National Library for Canada," 3.

40 CLA, Annual Conference, *Proceedings*, 1947: 13.

41 Ibid., 15.

42 A motion to establish a committee was passed at the 1947 conference, and the

committee, chaired by Waldon, reported to the 1948 conference (see CLA, Annual Conference, *Proceedings*, 1947: 15; *CLAB* 5 [July 1948]: 16-17). No minutes for this committee seem to have survived, but correspondence and other material in NA, CLA, Vol. 73, document the activities of CLA in this area.

43 The information that Kaye Lamb did not accept the position of dominion archivist until the prime minister agreed that it would include the "assignment of 'preparing the way for the organization of a national library'" was provided by Dr Lamb in a letter to Albert Bowron dated 10 June 1995.

44 Martha Shepard, reminiscences, 1994. Kaye Lamb recalls that Elizabeth Morton suggested Jean Lunn for the position of bibliographer (W. Kaye Lamb, reminiscences, 1994).

45 CLA, "The National Library of Canada."

46 Canada, Royal Commission on National Development in the Arts, Letters and Sciences, *Report*, 331.

47 *CLAB* 9 (Sept. 1952): 36.

48 Donnelly, *The National Library of Canada*, 66, 75, 79.

49 NA, CLA, 9-1, Executive Director, Reports to Council, 1947-52, Report, 28 Feb. 1949.

50 *CLAB* 8 (Nov. 1951): 76.

51 CLA, Annual Conference, *Proceedings*, 1954: 40, 41.

52 Robert H. Blackburn, reminiscences, 1994.

53 Mary Morton, letter to C.E. Clifford, 6 Sept. 1983; quoted in Clifford, "Elizabeth Homer Morton," 29.

54 NA, CLA, 9-1, Executive Secretary, Reports to Council, 1947-52, June Report [1948].

55 Roberta Wilson Weiner, reminiscences, 1994.

56 NA, CLA, 9-1, Executive Secretary, Reports to Council, 1947-52, Report, Nov. and Dec. 1948.

57 Ibid., Field Trip to the Maritime Provinces, Oct.-Nov. 1951.

58 NA, CLA, Vol. 1, Council and Board of Directors, Minutes, 20 June 1955.

59 NA, CLA, Vol. 64, Canadian Library Inquiry, 1960-1963, V.W. Clapp to E.H. Morton, 24 Sept. 1956.

60 Preisman, "In Memoriam."

61 "A Day in the Life of the CLA – ACB Executive Office," 450.

62 Joyce Rous Sowby, reminiscences, 1994.

63 Catherine Moyse Knowles, reminiscences, 1994. Evidence of these economies survive in the CLA archives. Carbon copies of correspondence, for example, were made on the backs of sheets recycled from the *Canadian Index*, reports, and other publications.

64 "CLA – ACB at Work," 312.

[65] Preisman, "In Memoriam."
[66] Ibid.
[67] Isabel Bradley, reminiscences, 1994.
[68] Preisman, "In Memoriam."
[69] Annita Wilson, reminiscences, 1994.
[70] Bassam, "Elizabeth Homer Morton," 257.
[71] Joyce Rous Sowby, reminiscences, 1994.
[72] Freda Waldon at the 1947 conference (CLA, Annual Conference, *Proceedings*, 1947: 14).

CHAPTER THREE

[1] CLA, *Constitution* [1947?], 3.
[2] Waldon, "The C.L.A. – The First Twenty Years," 23.
[3] CLA, *Supplement to Canadian Public Library Laws, 1947*, preface.
[4] Ibid.
[5] *CLAB* 8 (Nov. 1951): 75.
[6] A copy of the "Provisional Report, June 1952" on the Canadian library charter is in MTRL, TPL Papers, Box 26.
[7] CLA, *Suggested Standards of Service*, i.
[8] *CLAB* 8 (Nov. 1951): 77.
[9] CLA, *Suggested Standards of Service*, 12.
[10] *CLAB* 12 (Oct. 1955): 58.
[11] *Feliciter* 9, no. 3, pt. 1 (Nov. 1963): 8.
[12] NA, CLA, Vol. 2, Council and Board of Directors, Minutes, 25 June 1965.
[13] CLA, *Suggested Standards of Service*, 18; CLA, *Standards of Service* (1957), 11.
[14] *CLAB* 8 (Nov. 1951): 77.
[15] Waldon, "The C.L.A. – The First Twenty Years," 24-5.
[16] *CLAB* 5 (July 1948): 46. Just after the CLA conference, at the ALA convention in Buffalo, minimum salary scales were presented to the membership of the American organization, and this policy statement was published in the CLA *Bulletin* after the announcement of the Canadian committee in 1946 (see *CLAB* 3 [Oct. 1946]: 19).
[17] *CLAB* 5 (July 1948): 47.
[18] Ibid., 48.
[19] *CLAB* 6 (Jan. 1950): 144-5.
[20] "Classification of Positions and Salary Scale for Public Libraries in Canada, by Claude Aubry" was published as appendix 1 to the report of the salaries committee, 1949-50, in *CLAB* 7 (Sept. 1950): 59-61.

21 *Feliciter* 1, no. 3 (May 1956): 25.
22 *CLAB* 15 (Nov. 1958): 97.
23 CLA, *Salary Scales Recommended for Public Libraries, College and University Libraries in Canada*, 6.
24 CACUL, *A Draft Report on Position Classification*, 4.
25 *CLAB* 5 (July 1948): 48.
26 NA, CLA, Vol. 1, Council and Board of Directors, Minutes, 22 June 1954.
27 *CL* 17 (May 1961): 363.
28 *CLAB* 13 (Oct. 1956): 60.
29 *CLAB* 10 (June 1954): xvi.
30 *CLAB* 11 (Oct. 1954): 54.
31 John M. Marshall, interview with the author, 23 Nov. 1994.
32 *CLAB* 13 (Oct. 1956): 60.
33 John H. Archer, reminiscences, 1994.
34 *CLAB* 13 (Oct. 1956): 61-2.
35 Robert H. Blackburn, reminiscences, 1994.
36 CLA, Annual Conference, *Proceedings*, 1954: 45.
37 I am grateful to Diane Henderson of the Faculty of Information Studies Library, University of Toronto, for arranging for me to view a print of this film.
38 *Feliciter* 3, no. 4 (Dec. 1957): 23.
39 NA, CLA, Vol. 1, Council and Board of Directors, Minutes, 19-20 June 1947.
40 Chatwin, *Investigation Report*, 7, inside front cover. The policy was reaffirmed at the 1958 conference (see *CLAB* 15 [Sept. 1958]: 71).
41 Robert H. Blackburn, reminiscences, 1994.
42 Bruce Peel, reminiscences, 1994.
43 Chatwin, *Investigation Report*, inside front cover.
44 *CL* 17 (May 1961): 336.
45 NA, CLA, Vol. 1, Council and Board of Directors, Minutes, 20-24 Nov. 1959; *CL* 17 (May 1961): 337.
46 *CLAB* 12 (Oct. 1955): 61.
47 *Feliciter* 1, no. 3 (May 1956): 26.
48 *Feliciter* 2, no. 2 (March 1957): 7.
49 *CL* 17 (May 1961): 356.
50 *Feliciter* 4, no. 5 (Jan. 1959): 19-20.
51 CLA, Annual Conference, *Proceedings*, 1965: 23.
52 Waldon, "The C.L.A. – The First Twenty Years," 25.
53 *CLAB* 7 (May 1951): 244.
54 *CLAB* 11 (June 1955): 344; see also *CLAB* 9 (May 1953): 186.
55 In 1965 Elizabeth Morton was forced to report to the board of directors that

when the association had been asked to file with the Royal Commission on Bilingualism and Biculturalism all the briefs it had presented to royal commissions between 1944 and 1965, some could not be found and a few were available in summary form only (see NA, CLA, 9-2, Executive Director, Reports to Council, 1954-66, Letter, 13 April 1965).

56 Marion C. Wilson, reminiscences, 1994.

57 *CLAB* 13 (Aug. 1956): 13.

58 *CLAB* 15 (Sept. 1958): 70; see also *CLAB* 13 (Aug. 1956): 13.

59 Robert H. Blackburn, reminiscences, 1994.

60 *CLAB* 12 (Oct. 1955): 75.

61 Ibid., 75-6.

62 Ibid., 60.

63 *CLAB* 15 (Sept. 1958): 69-70.

64 *CL* 24 (May 1968): 625.

65 Ibid., 626.

66 The establishment of a committee on intellectual freedom had been one of the resolutions at the 1948 conference, but nothing seems to have resulted in the short term from this proposal (see *CLAB* 5 [July 1948]: 50).

67 *CLAB* 10 (July 1953): viii-ix. According to some later accounts, this committee was established in 1950, but the Council minutes for September 1952 record that no chair had yet been appointed (see NA, CLA, Vol. 1, Council and Board of Directors, Minutes, 27-29 Sept. 1952).

68 *CLAB* 10 (July 1953): ix.

69 *CLAB* 15 (Sept. 1958): 69.

70 NA, CLA, Vol. 2, Council and Board of Directors, Minutes, 2-4 Nov. 1962.

71 *CL* 23 (Nov. 1966): 193.

72 Archer, "This Freedom," 329.

CHAPTER FOUR

1 *CLAB* 15 (Sept. 1958): 73.

2 NA, CLA, 9-2, Executive Director, Reports to Council, 1954-66, E.H. Morton to Council, 24 Oct. 1958.

3 *Feliciter* 7, no. 1 (Sept. 1961): 4. This was an unusually high registration for CLA. Of a total membership of just under 2,000 in 1960, from 350 to 650 might normally attend an annual conference, depending on where it was held.

4 NA, CLA, Vol. 1, Council and Board of Directors, Montreal Conference Advisory Committee, Minutes, 16 March 1960.

5 NA, CLA, Vol. 1, Council and Board of Directors, Minutes, 6 Nov. 1960.

6 Ibid.

[7] *Feliciter* 7, no. 1 (Sept. 1961): 7, 3-4.
[8] Waldon, "The C.L.A. – The First Twenty Years," 30.
[9] Robert H. Blackburn, reminiscences, 1994.
[10] Neal R. Harlow, reminiscences, 1994.
[11] Dean W. Halliwell, reminiscences, 1994.
[12] Martha Shepard, reminiscences, 1994.
[13] *CL* 17 (Sept. 1960): 68.
[14] *CL* 17 (Nov. 1960): 141.
[15] NA, CLA, Vol. 1, Council and Board of Directors, Minutes, 8 Nov. 1960.
[16] *Feliciter* 6, no. 5 (Jan. 1961): 13b.
[17] Donnelly, *The National Library of Canada*, 153.
[18] *Feliciter* 7, no. 11-12 (July-Aug. 1962): 2. See also NA, CLA, Vol. 73, National Library, 1960-63, Robert H. Hamilton to John G. Diefenbaker, 29 June 1962 (copy).
[19] *Feliciter* 7, no. 11-12 (July-Aug. 1962): 2; NA, CLA, Vol. 73, National Library, 1960-63, J.G. Diefenbaker to R.H. Hamilton, 4 July 1962.
[20] CLA, *The Present State of Library Service in Canada*, pt. I B, "Executive Office," 15. The Toronto Public Library had begun an index to business and industrial magazines in 1958, which was to be considered a pilot project for a section of the *Canadian Index*, but this index was discontinued in December 1962.
[21] Ibid., 17.
[22] *CLAB* 15 (May 1959): 275.
[23] NA, CLA, Vol. 63, Canada Council, Correspondence with, 1956-58, Morton to the Canada Council, 3 Dec. 1958.
[24] Ibid., Morton to Coughlin, 17 Sept. 1957.
[25] Ibid., Morton to Dawson, 23 Feb. 1960.
[26] *CL* 24 (Nov. 1967): 252.
[27] NA, CLA, Vol. 1, Council and Board of Directors, Minutes, 15 June 1957.
[28] *Feliciter* 3, no. 10, pt. 2 (June 1958): 9.
[29] Ibid., 11.
[30] Morton, "Canadian Library Association," *ELIS*, 181-2.
[31] Public libraries would eventually become a division of the restructured CLA in 1972 (see chapter 5).
[32] *CL* 20 (Jan. 1964): 190.
[33] *Feliciter* 8, no. 9-10, pt. 2 (May-June 1963): CT2.
[34] *CLAB* 12 (Oct. 1955): 58.
[35] NA, CLA, 9-2, Executive Director, Reports to Council, 1954-66, Report for Oct. to Jan., 1964-65. Elizabeth Morton's title was changed from executive secretary to executive director in the 1960-61 year.

[36] Ibid., Report for May-Oct. 1963.
[37] *Feliciter* 9, no. 9-10, pt. 2 (May-June 1964): 4.
[38] NA, CLA, 9-2, Executive Director, Reports to Council, 1954-66, Letter, 1 Oct. 1963.
[39] NA, CLA, Vol. 2, Council and Board of Directors, Minutes, 27 Oct. 1963.
[40] NA, CLA, 9-2, Executive Director, Reports to Council, 1954-66, Letter, 25 Nov. 1965.
[41] Robert H. Blackburn, reminiscences, 1994.
[42] Dean W. Halliwell, reminiscences, 1994.
[43] W. Kaye Lamb, reminiscences, 1994.
[44] Bruce Peel, reminiscences, 1994.
[45] NA, CLA, Vol. 2, Council and Board of Directors, file for 1964, Letter from the Executive Director to Council, undated.
[46] The item appeared in *Feliciter* 8, no. 11 (July 1963): 16. The edited copy is in NA, CLA, Vol. 64, Committee on Canadian Library Resources Survey, 1957-63.
[47] "Morton, Elizabeth Homer," *Current Biography Yearbook*, 325.
[48] *Feliciter* 9, no. 9-10, pt. 2 (May-June 1964): 6.
[49] NA, CLA, Vol. 2, Council and Board of Directors, Minutes, 16-17 Oct. 1964.
[50] NA, CLA, 9-2, Executive Director, Reports to Council, 1954-66, Letter to the Directors, 26 Feb. 1965.
[51] Ibid., Letter to the Directors, 13 April 1965. The low figure for the Xerox machine is perhaps explained by the fact that it would be a rental rather than a purchase. In her annual report for 1964-65, Morton stated that the office was renting a Xerox 914 (see *Feliciter* 10, no. 8-9, pt. 2 [April-May 1965]: 4.)
[52] *CLAB* 15 (May 1959): 272.
[53] Dean W. Halliwell, reminiscences, 1994.
[54] *Feliciter* 10, no. 8-9, pt. 2 (April-May 1965): 4.
[55] "A Day in the Life of the CLA – ACB Executive Office," 452. Subsequent quotations in this chapter are from this source at the pages indicated in the text.

CHAPTER FIVE

[1] *Feliciter* 11, no. 3 (Nov. 1965): 1. Emphasis in the original.
[2] Ibid.
[3] CLA, Annual Conference, *Proceedings*, 1965: 23.
[4] Ibid., 21-2.
[5] NA, CLA, Vol. 2, Council and Board of Directors, Agenda, 30-31 Oct. 1965, 3.
[6] *Feliciter* 11, no. 4 (Dec. 1965): 28. For apparently the first time, the minutes of this council meeting were published in *Feliciter*.

7 Ibid., 46.
8 Ibid., 49.
9 Ibid., 50.
10 Ibid., 51.
11 Ibid.
12 CLA, Annual Conference, *Proceedings*, 1965: 23-4. Bruce Peel recorded in his journal that Castell spoke "eloquently, needlessly, and certainly tactlessly" (Peel, reminiscences, 1994). Basil Stuart-Stubbs recalls that there were "many prominent Quebec librarians at that conference, some of whom walked out. I was shocked and angered by Castell's words, but my emotions were mild compared to those of the despairing Quebec librarians to whom I spoke after the meeting. There was simply no way to console them" (Stuart-Stubbs, reminiscences, 1994).
13 *CL* 20 (1963): 60-1.
14 Ibid., 62.
15 Ibid., 63.
16 NA, CLA, Vol. 2, Council and Board of Directors, Minutes (verbatim), 30 Oct. 1965.
17 Stuart-Stubbs, "The Librarians of Québec and the Canadian Library Association," 373.
18 When Desrochers pointed this fact out to Elizabeth Morton, she invited him to contribute his comments, which were included as "The Library Inquiry and the A.C.B.L.F." in *The Present State of Library Service in Canada*, Part I A and Part II A.
19 *Feliciter* 12, no. 11-12 (July-Aug. 1967): unnumbered page. The CLA Council did not discuss this memorandum until its fall meeting, and its response was to form the Council advisory group, made up of representatives of the regional associations with which CLA was affiliated.
20 Stuart-Stubbs, "The Librarians of Québec and the Canadian Library Association," 382.
21 Amy M. Hutcheson, reminiscences, 1994.
22 Stuart-Stubbs, "The Librarians of Québec and the Canadian Library Association," 383.
23 Basil Stuart-Stubbs, reminiscences, 1994.
24 Robert H. Blackburn, reminiscences, 1994.
25 John H. Archer, reminiscences, 1994.
26 Dean W. Halliwell, reminiscences, 1994.
27 Marion C. Wilson, reminiscences, 1994.
28 June E. Munro, reminiscences, 1994.

[29] Basil Stuart-Stubbs, reminiscences, 1994.

[30] CLA, Annual Conference, *Proceedings*, 1966: 124.

[31] NA, CLA, Vol. 63, Canadian Library Research and Development Council, Correspondence, 1946-60, Letters Patent, 24 Oct. 1957 (photocopy).

[32] Ibid., G.A. Brakeley & Co. Ltd., "A Report on Fund-Raising Potential for the Canadian Library Research Foundation, Toronto, Ontario, March 1963," 11.

[33] Ibid.

[34] Ibid., 12.

[35] NA, CLA, Vol. 63, Canadian Library Research and Development Council, Correspondence, 1963-67, Report of the President (undated and incomplete).

[36] *CL* 24 (March 1968): 515.

[37] NA, CLA, Vol. 64, Study of Canadian Libraries, Correspondence, 1967-68, Katharine Ball to Amy Hutcheson, 25 April 1967. The CLRDC does seem to have become moribund after its proposal to be involved in the study was rejected.

[38] Ibid., John Archer to Katharine Ball, 1 May 1967.

[39] *CL* 24 (May 1968): 627.

[40] NA, CLA, Vol. 64, Study of Canadian Libraries, Correspondence, memoranda, 1967-70, Report of the Chairman to the Steering Committee [May 1968].

[41] NA, CLA, Vol. 3, Council and Board of Directors, Minutes, 28 Jan. 1969. Report published in *Feliciter* 14, no. 7-9 (March-May 1969), pt. 2 (annual reports): 55-8.

[42] NA, CLA, 9-2, Executive Director, Reports to Council, 1954-66, Letter, 23 March 1966.

[43] *CL* 24 (Nov. 1967): 245.

[44] Ibid., 239-40.

[45] Ibid., 218-9. Some details in this section have been added from *IFLA News*, no. 22 (Oct. 1967): 2-3.

[46] *Feliciter* 12, no. 7 (March 1967): 49.

[47] *CL* 23 (Nov. 1966): 208.

[48] Ibid.

[49] Ibid., 208-9.

[50] Ibid., 211.

[51] Ibid.

[52] *Feliciter* 14, no. 7-9 (March-May 1969), pt. 2 (annual reports): 46.

[53] Ibid., 47. The change in name from *Canadian Library* had been an attempt to qualify the publication as second-class mail. However, it was unsuccessful, and as of 1 April 1969 there would be a significant increase in the cost of mailing the journal to subscribers.

[54] Ibid., 50.

[55] NA, CLA, Vol. 3, Council and Board of Directors, Editorial and Publications Policy Committee, Report to Council, November 1970.
[56] *CL* 23 (May 1967): 496.
[57] *Feliciter* 13, no. 1-3 (Sept.-Nov. 1967): 14.
[58] *Feliciter* no. 14, no. 4-6 (Dec. 1968-Jan./Feb. 1969): 7.
[59] The chairs of relevant committees were invited early in 1969 to form a committee to consider the formation of a public libraries association (see NA, CLA, Vol. 3, Council and Board of Directors, Committee on Committees, Report, 21 Feb. 1969). A proposed constitution was published in *Feliciter* in January 1970. However, the Canadian Association of Public Libraries did not gain section status until June 1972, after the restructuring of CLA had been approved (see *Feliciter* 18, no. 5 [July-Aug. 1972]: 2).
[60] CLA, Annual Conference, *Proceedings*, 1969: 83.
[61] Moon, "Newfoundland Revisited," 2563.
[62] *Feliciter* 15, no. 1-2 (Sept.-Oct. 1969): 1.
[63] Ibid.
[64] Ibid., 3. Subsequent quotations in this section are from the same source at the pages indicated in the text. The comments were published anonymously, but the original letters are in NA, CLA, 5-2, Council Advisory Group.
[65] *CLJ* 27 (May-June 1970): 224.
[66] *CLJ* 27 (Nov.-Dec. 1970): 416.
[67] Ibid.
[68] Ibid.
[69] NA, CLA, Vol. 3, Council and Board of Directors, Minutes, 21, 25-6 June 1970.
[70] *Simon Fraser University Information Bulletin: Monthly Report to Library Staff and Faculty* 5, no. 10 (June 1970): unpaged. I am grateful to Bruce Peel for tracking down the source of this account of the 1970 conference, a copy of which appears in the correspondence file for his presidency in NA, CLA, Vol. 6.
[71] CLA, Annual Conference, *Proceedings*, 1970: 62.
[72] NA, CLA, Vol. 3, Council and Board of Directors, Minutes, 21, 25-6 June 1970.
[73] *Feliciter* 17, no. 5-6 (May-June 1971): 4.
[74] The objectives, as amended by the CLA membership at the annual conference in 1971, were published in *Feliciter* 17, no. 7-8 (July-August 1971): 25-8; and *CLJ* 28 (Nov.-Dec. 1971): 454-6.
[75] NA, CLA, Vol. 4, Council and Board of Directors, Minutes, 26-27 March 1971.
[76] A resolution presented at the 1970 conference by the Canadian Library Trustees' Association had deplored the lack of representation for public library trustees in the federation proposed by the CAG and resolved that the CLTA be a constituent society of any restructured CLA (see CLA, Annual Conference, *Proceedings*, 1970: 61).

77 NA, CLA, Vol. 4, Council and Board of Directors, Preliminary Report of the Structural Committee to Council, 19 Oct. 1971.
78 *Feliciter* 18, no. 5 (July-Aug. 1972): 1. The final report of the ad hoc committee on structure appears in CLA, Annual Conference, *Proceedings*, 1972: 28-32.
79 NA, CLA, Vol. 3, Council and Board of Directors, Minutes, 30 Sept. 1967.
80 *CLJ* 29 (May-June 1972): 217.
81 Dean W. Halliwell, reminiscences, 1994.
82 Bruce Peel, reminiscences, 1994.
83 Basil Stuart-Stubbs, reminiscences, 1994.

CHAPTER SIX

1 NA, CLA, Vol. 2, Council and Board of Directors, Minutes, 27 Oct. 1963.
2 Ibid., Minutes, 1 Feb. 1965.
3 *CL* 23 (Nov. 1966): 235.
4 NA, CLA, Vol. 2, Council and Board of Directors, Minutes, 16 June 1967.
5 Ibid., Minutes, 23 June 1967.
6 Marion C. Wilson, reminiscences, 1994.
7 Ibid.
8 *CL* 24 (Nov. 1967): 279.
9 *CL* 24 (March 1968): 514. In 1961 he had published a short article entitled "Some Reflections on Libraries in Canada" in *Stechert-Hafner Book News*.
10 Marion C. Wilson, reminiscences, 1994.
11 NA, CLA, Vol. 3, Council and Board of Directors, Minutes, 17 Feb. 1968.
12 Marion C. Wilson, reminiscences, 1994.
13 Hutcheson, "Elizabeth Homer Morton," 10.
14 Ibid., 17.
15 Florence Murray, letter to Constance E. Clifford, 17 Oct. 1983; quoted in Clifford, "Elizabeth Homer Morton," 42.
16 Blackburn, "Canadian Library Association," 30.
17 Hutcheson, "Elizabeth Homer Morton," 9.
18 NA, CLA, Vol. 2, Council and Board of Directors, Minutes, 23 June 1967.
19 Waldon, "The C.L.A. – The First Twenty Years," 27.
20 NA, CLA, Vol. 2, Council and Board of Directors, Minutes, 23 June 1967.
21 Marion C. Wilson, reminiscences, 1994.
22 Basil Stuart-Stubbs, reminiscences, 1994.
23 Marion C. Wilson, reminiscences, 1994.
24 John H. Archer, reminiscences, 1994.
25 Ibid.

26 June E. Munro, reminiscences, 1994.
27 Dean W. Halliwell, reminiscences, 1994.
28 Hutcheson, "Elizabeth Homer Morton," 9.
29 June E. Munro, reminiscences, 1994.
30 Hutcheson, "Elizabeth Homer Morton," 12.
31 Ibid., 13.
32 Ibid.
33 Martha Shepard, reminiscences, 1994.
34 M.E.P. Henderson, letter to Constance E. Clifford, 16 Sept. 1983; quoted in Clifford, "Elizabeth Homer Morton," 29.
35 Hutcheson, "Elizabeth Homer Morton," 17.
36 John H. Archer, reminiscences, 1994.
37 Bruce Peel, telephone conversation with Constance E. Clifford, 11 Aug. 1983; quoted in Clifford, "Elizabeth Homer Morton," 28.
38 Bassam, "Elizabeth Homer Morton," 256.
39 Wilson, "In Memoriam."
40 Isabel Bradley, reminiscences, 1994.
41 Waldon, "The C.L.A. – The First Twenty Years," 35.
42 Howard, "Sir George Williams University Confers ..."
43 NLC, Library Development Office, E.H. Morton file, Morton, circular letter, Christmas 1975. The papers of Sarah and John Morton are in the archives of the Presbyterian Church of Canada, Knox College, Toronto. A microfilm made by CLA is at the NA.
44 Dean W. Halliwell, reminiscences, 1994.
45 NA, CLA, Vol. 4, Council and Board of Directors, Minutes, 25 and 28 March 1971. In fact, he later claimed that "the Association would probably not now exist if there had not been a lawyer occupying the position" (see ibid., Minutes, 19, 24-5 June 1971).
46 Marion C. Wilson, reminiscences, 1994.
47 Dean W. Halliwell, reminiscences, 1994.
48 Isabel Bradley, reminiscences, 1994.
49 Dean W. Halliwell, reminiscences, 1994.
50 Robert H. Blackburn, reminiscences, 1994.
51 Moon, "Newfoundland Revisited," 2563.
52 Marion C. Wilson, reminiscences, 1994.
53 Ibid.
54 Amy M. Hutcheson, reminiscences, 1994.
55 Erik J. Spicer, reminiscences, 1994.
56 Bruce Peel, reminiscences, 1994.

57 Amy M. Hutcheson, reminiscences, 1994.
58 NA, CLA, Vol. 5, Council Advisory Group, Martha Shepard to Council and CAG, 16 April 1971.
59 Martha Shepard, reminiscences, 1994.
60 NA, CLA, Vol. 7, Re: C. Currie, Currie to Martha Shepard, 12 Aug. 1971.
61 "U.S. Denies Work Permit," 507.
62 "Labor Dept. Nixes Appointment."
63 "Currie Okayed for Virginia Post."
64 Bruce Peel, reminiscences, 1994.
65 Basil Stuart-Stubbs, reminiscences, 1994.
66 John H. Archer, reminiscences, 1994.
67 Dean W. Halliwell, reminiscences, 1994.

Bibliography

ARCHIVAL AND UNPUBLISHED SOURCES

Metropolitan Toronto Reference Library, Baldwin Room
Toronto Public Library Papers. This collection includes correspondence with Charles R. Sanderson and R.D. Hilton Smith relating to CLA matters.

National Archives of Canada (NA), Manuscript Division
Canadian Library Association Papers (MG 28, I 197). This collection, extending to approximately 21.5 metres, covers the period 1946-73, with some material from early and later periods. It is made up of donations from CLA in 1973 and 1986, Mary Morton in 1977, and the National Library of Canada in 1985 and 1987. Of particular importance for this study were the following files:
Volumes 1-5. Council and Board of Directors. Agenda, minutes, transcripts, reports. 1946-73.
Volume 5. Council Advisory Group. Correspondence, proposal. 1968-72.
Volumes 6-7. Presidents. Correspondence, memoranda. 1967-72.
Volumes 9-10. Executive Director. Correspondence, memoranda. 1947-72.
Volumes 87-91. Canadian Library Council. Miscellaneous files. 1940-47.
The collection is referenced in the notes as: NA, CLA, followed by the box (volume) and file number, the file title, and the item cited.

National Library of Canada (NLC), Library Development Office
Untitled typescript biography of Elizabeth Homer Morton in the E.H. Morton file. This document was apparently written about 1961 by someone who knew her well, possibly her sister Mary Morton, and may have been prepared in connection with the shorter entry on Elizabeth Morton that appeared in *Current Biography* that year (see below).

Presbyterian Church in Canada Archives, Knox College, Toronto
Morton, John and Sarah Etter (Silver). Correspondence, diaries, notes, etc. 1856-1912. Microfilm copy in the National Archives of Canada.

Personal Reminiscences
At the request of the Ex Libris Association, reminiscences were provided by the following individuals in 1994:
John H. Archer, Eva S. Balogh, Robert H. Blackburn, Isabel Lee Bradley, Harry Campbell, Dean W. Halliwell, Amy M. Hutcheson, Catherine Moyse Knowles, W. Kaye Lamb (interviewed by Basil Stuart-Stubbs), June E. Munro, Neal Harlow, Bruce Peel, Martha Shepard, Joyce Rous Sowby, Erik J. Spicer, Basil Stuart-Stubbs, Roberta Wilson Weiner, Annita Wilson, Marion C. Wilson.
The originals are in the possession of the association.

SERIAL PUBLICATIONS

Canadian Library. 16-25 (1960-68). Continued by *Canadian Library Journal.*
Canadian Library Association. *Annual Reports.* 1948/49-1971/72. Some issued as part 2 of the spring issue of *Feliciter.*
— *Bulletin.* 3-16 (1946-60). Continued the Canadian Library Council *Bulletin*; continued by *Canadian Library.* Of particular importance for this study were the tenth anniversary number (published in June 1955), the accounts of the years 1955-60 (published in the May 1961 issue) and 1960-66 (May 1967), and the description of projects and committees, 1960-67 (May 1968).
— *Occasional Papers.* 1-79 (1953-70).
— Annual Conference. *Proceedings.* 1946-72. Proceedings for some annual conferences, including the annual general meeting, appear wholly or in part in the fall issues of *CLAB* and *CL.*
Canadian Library Council. *Bulletin.* 1-2 (1944-46). Continued by the Canadian Library Association *Bulletin.*
Canadian Library Horizons. 1-4 (1963-67). Ottawa.
Canadian Library Journal. 26-9 (1969-72). Continued *Canadian Library.*
Canadian Periodical Index. Ottawa: Canadian Library Association. Originally published as *Canadian Index: A Guide to Canadian Periodicals and Films*; later as *Canadian Index to Periodicals and Documentary Films.* First monthly number issued January 1948; annual cumulations from 1949.
Feliciter. 1 (1956)-18 (1972).

OTHER PUBLISHED SOURCES

Archer, John H. "Canadian Library Association – Association Canadienne des

Bibliothèques." *Encyclopedia Americana* (1984) 5: 514.
— "This Freedom." *CL* 19 (March 1963): 329-30.
Arneaud, John D. "Mission to Trinidad." *Chronicle-Herald* (Halifax). 27 March 1992.
"Association Activities, 1946-1955." *CLAB* 11 (June 1955): 273-8.
"At a Glance." *CL* 17 (May 1961): 382-95. CLA sections, committees, and conferences, 1946-60.
Bassam, Bertha. "Elizabeth Homer Morton: Librarian, Administrator, Author, Editor." *CLJ* 35 (Aug. 1978): 253-7.
— *The Faculty of Library Science, University of Toronto, and Its Predecessors 1911-1972.* Toronto: Faculty of Library Science in association with the Library Science Alumni Association, 1978.
Blackburn, Robert H. "Canadian Library Association." *Stechert-Hafner Book News* 14 (Nov. 1959): 29-30.
— "The Job So Far." In "Microfilm Section," *CLAB* 10 (July 1953): ii-iii.
Bletcher, Hazel. "On the Formation of a Canadian Library Association: Paper Given before the Alberta Library Association." *CLCB* 2, no. 2 (Dec. 1945): 19.
Bothwell, Robert, Ian Drummond, and John English. *Canada since 1945: Power, Politics, and Provincialism.* Rev. ed. Toronto: University of Toronto Press, 1989.
Bradley, Isabel, et al. "Projects, 1 September 1955-31 August 1960." *CL* 17 (May 1961): 303-10.
"By Way of Introduction." *ALAB* 21 (Aug. 1927): 223.
"CLA – ACB at Work: Headquarters, Sections, Projects, Committees." *CLAB* 11 (June 1955): 309-64.
"The CLA – ACB Projects, 1 September 1960-31 August 1967." *CL* 24 (May 1968): 582-9.
Canada. Royal Commission on National Development in the Arts, Letters and Sciences. *Report.* Ottawa: King's Printer, 1951.
Canadian Association of College and University Libraries. *A Draft Report on Position Classifications & Salary Scales in Canadian Academic Libraries.* Calgary, 1966.
Canadian Biographies: Artists and Authors. 3 vols. [Ottawa] Canadian Library Association, 1948-52.
Canadian Book Centre. *Report of Operations, 1948-1950.* [s.l., 1955].
"The Canadian Book Centre." *CLAB* 5 (Nov. 1948): 114.
Canadian Library Association. *And Canada's National Library.* Ottawa, 1961.
— *Canadian Library Directory, 1947-1948.* Reference Publication No. 3. Ottawa: Canadian Library Association, [1948]. Subsequently published biennial ly with annual supplements; some issues published in *CL.*
— *Canadian Public Library Laws, 1946.* Reference Publication No. 2. Victoria, B.C.: King's Printer, 1947. And *Supplement to Canadian Public Library Laws, 1947* (Reference Publication No. 2A, Victoria, B.C., 1948).

— "CLA – ACB Brief for Fowler Commission." *CLAB* 13 (Aug. 1956): 12-5.
— *Constitution.* [1947?].
— "Interim Salary Scale Recommended for Public Libraries in Canada." *CLAB* 10 (Dec. 1953): 134-5.
— *Library Finance: Speeches, Proceedings and Recommendations of a Day of Special Study during the Eleventh Annual Conference.* Occasional Paper No. 12. Ottawa, 1956.
— "Memorandum of Agreement (General By-laws of Corporation as Set Forth in Letters Patent)." [1947]. Mimeographed.
— "The National Library of Canada, Its Eventual Character and Scope: A Brief Submitted to the Chairman and Members of the Royal Commission on National Development in the Arts, Letters, and Sciences, by the Canadian Library Association – Association Canadienne des Bibliothèques, August 18th, 1949." *CLAB* 6 (Sept. 1949): 36-8.
— *100 Library Years in Canada 1851-1951: A Picture Book of Libraries.* Ottawa, 1951.
— *The Present State of Library Service in Canada: A Program of Inquiry for 1960/61.* Part I A and Part II A. Ottawa, [1961].
— "Professional Qualifications for Librarians in Canada: Official Statement from the Council of the Canadian Library Association – Association Canadienne des Bibliothèques." *Feliciter* 6, no. 1 (Sept. 1960): 21. Also issued as an offprint.
— *Retirement Plan for Members of Canadian Library Association / Association Canadienne des Bibliothèques.* Ottawa, 1958.
— *Salary Scales Recommended for Public Libraries, College and University Libraries in Canada.* [s.l., 1957]
— *Standards of Service for Public Libraries in Canada.* [Ottawa, 1957, 1962]. Published in French as *Normes de service pour les bibliothèques au Canada.*
— *Suggested Standards of Service for Public Libraries in Canada.* Ottawa [1955].
— *Working Conditions in Canadian Public Libraries.* 1962, 1966. *1966 Working Conditions ...* (1967) published as Occasional Paper No. 69.
— Committee to Consider the Section Organization of CLA – ACB. "Interim Report, for Discussion at Quebec." *Feliciter* 3, no. 10, pt. 2 (June 1958): 9-11.
— Council Advisory Group. "Feasibility Study for a Canadian Library Association Federation." *Feliciter* 14, no. 10-12 (June-Aug. 1969): enclosure.
— Microfilm Committee. *Canadian Newspapers on Microfilm: Catalogue.* Compiledby the Microfilm Committee of the Canadian Library Association under the supervision of Sheila A. Egoff. Ottawa, 1959.
— Special Committee on Microfilming. "A Report." *CLAB* 3 (April 1947): 97-8.
Canadian Library Association et al. "A National Library for Canada: A Brief Presented to the Government of Canada ... December, 1946." *OLR* 31 (Feb.

1947): 3-10. A condensation appears in *CLAB* 3 (Feb. 1947): 69-73.
"Canadian Library Association." *ALAB* 21 (Aug. 1927): 226.
"Canadian Library Association: Change of Name." *Feliciter* 14, no. 7-9 (March-May 1969): 2-3.
"Canadian Library Consultants." *ALAB* 34 (Dec. 1940): 716.
Canadian Library Council. "Events of 1945-46." *CLCB* 2, no. 1 (Oct. 1945): 1.
— *Libraries in the Life of the Canadian Nation: An Interim Report Presented to the Organizational Conference of the Canadian Library Association by the Canadian Library Council, Inc., June, 1946.* Part I, Public Libraries. [Ottawa, 1946].
— *Library Service for Canada: A Brief.* [Ottawa], 1944. Brief to the House of Commons Special Committee on Reconstruction and Re-establishment, chaired by James Gray Turgeon.
"Canadian Library Council." *ALAB* 35 (Sept. 1941): P31.
"Canadian Library Council: Report of Progress, Milwaukee, June 25, 1942." *ALAB* 36 (Aug. 1942): 523.
"Canadian Library Council Formed." *ALAB* 28 (Aug. 1934): 461-2.
Chatwin, Dorothy B. *Investigation Report on Library Education.* Education for Librarianship, Study No. 1. Ottawa: Canadian Library Association, 1955.
Clifford, Constance E. "Elizabeth Homer Morton: A Biography." MLS non-thesis project, University of Alberta, 1983. Copy in the National Library ofCanada.
"Clifford Currie ..." *College and Research Libraries News,* no. 7 (July-Aug. 1978): 207-8.
Commission of Enquiry, John Ridington, chairman. *Libraries in Canada: A Study of Library Conditions and Needs.* Toronto: Ryerson Press; Chicago: American Library Association, 1933.
"Committees, 1 September 1960-31 August 1967." *CL* 24 (May 1968): 590-629.
Currie, Clifford. "Some Reflections on Libraries in Canada." *Stechert-Hafner Book News* 16 (Sept. 1961): 1-3.
"Currie Okayed for Virginia Post." *Wilson Library Bulletin* 53 (May 1979): 661.
"A Day in the Life of the CLA – ACB Executive Office." *CL* 21 (May 1965): 450-60.
"Deaths ... Elizabeth Homer Morton ..." *LJ* 102 (1 Sept. 1977): 1713.
Desrochers, Edmond E. "Canadian Library Education and Certification." *ALAB* 54 (April 1960): 310-2.
The Development of the New Brunswick Legislative Library, 1841-1991. Fredericton: Legislative Library, 1991.
"Diagrams and Statistics." *CL* 17 (May 1961): 338-43. CLA membership, receipts and disbursements, and the microfilm project, 1946-60.
Donnelly, F. Dolores. *The National Library of Canada: A Historical Analysis of the Forces Which Contributed to Its Establishment and to the Identification of Its Role and*

Responsibilities. Ottawa: Canadian Library Association, 1973.
Donovan, R.M. "Working Conditions in Canadian Libraries." *CLAB* 15 (Nov. 1958): 97-110.
Egoff, Sheila A. "Read It on Microfilm." *ALAB* 54 (April 1960): 286.
Elliot, Helen, ed. *Fate, Hope and Editorials: Contemporary Accounts and Opinions in the Newspapers, 1862-73, Microfilmed by the CLA/ACB Microfilm Project.* Ottawa: Canadian Library Association, 1967.
"Events of 1945-46." *CLCB* 2, no. 1 (Oct. 1945): 1.
Foley, David W. "The C.L.A. as Publisher." In *Librarianship in Canada, 1946 to 1967: Essays in Honour of Elizabeth Homer Morton*, ed. Bruce Peel, 38-45. Victoria, B.C.: Printed for the Canadian Library Association by the Morriss Printing Co., 1968.
"Forbes, His Honour James Gordon." In *The Canadian Men and Women of the Time: A Hand-book of Canadian Biography*, by Henry James Morgan. Toronto: W. Briggs, 1898, 1912.
"From Council to Association." *CLAB* 3 (Oct. 1946): 1, 17.
Gill, Margaret. "C.L.C. to C.L.A." In *Librarianship in Canada, 1946 to 1967: Essays in Honour of Elizabeth Homer Morton*, ed. Bruce Peel, 11-19. Victoria, B.C.: Printed for the Canadian Library Association by the Morriss Printing Co., 1968.
Hamilton, Robert M. "The Newspaper Microfilming Project." *CLAB* 4 (Feb. 1948): 89-93.
Henderson, George Fletcher. *Federal Royal Commissions in Canada, 1867-1966: A Checklist.* Toronto: University of Toronto Press, 1967.
Hilton Smith, R.D. "Rising to the Occasion." *CLAB* 7 (May 1951): 217-22.
Howard, Helen. "Sir George Williams University Confers Honorary Degree on Miss Elizabeth H. Morton." Quebec Library Association, *Newsletter* 13, no. 1 (Jan.-March 1971): 9.
Hutcheson, Amy M. "Elizabeth Homer Morton, CLA – ACB Executive Director 1946-1968." *CL* 25 (1968): 8-17.
Jenkins, Kathleen R. "Books and the Sales Tax." *CLAB* 9 (Nov. 1952): 100-1.
"Labor Dept. Nixes Appointment of Oxford Librarian at W&M." *LJ* 103 (1 Nov. 1978): 2158.
Lamb, W. Kaye. "Elizabeth Morton: Gaiety, Imagination and Patience." *Feliciter* 23, no. 7-8 (July-Aug. 1977): 1, 3.
"Librarian Mourned." *Evening Times Globe* (Saint John, N.B.), 12 July 1977.
"Library Associations of Canada 1900-1946." *CLAB* 11 (June 1955): 270-2.
Lomer, Gerhard R. "Background of the Canadian L.A." *LJ* 71 (1 Sept. 1946): 1107-10.
"Microfilm Section." *CLAB* 10 (July 1953): 64, i-xvi, 65-9.
"Montreal Conference, A.L.A.: Jottings by the Way." *OLR* 18 (Aug. 1934): 108-11.

Moon, Eric. "Newfoundland Revisited." *LJ* 94 (July 1969): 2562-6.
Morton, Elizabeth Homer. "ALA-CLA Liaison." *Stechert-Hafner Book News* 14 (Nov. 1959): 29-31.
— "The Association and Tenure." *CLAB* 13 (Oct. 1956): 59-60.
— "Books to Delight." *CL* 24 (Sept. 1967): 145-8.
— "The Canadian and the American Library Associations." *ALAB* 54 (April 1960): 282-5.
— "Canadian Books Abroad." *CLJ* 27 (Sept.-Oct. 1970): 366-7.
— "Canadian Library Association." In *Encyclopedia of Library and Information Science*, ed. Allen Kent and Harold Lancour, 4: 170-92. New York: Marcel Dekker, 1970.
— "The Canadian Library Association – Association Canadienne des Bibliothèques." In *Encyclopedia Americana* (1965) 5: 478i-j.
— "The Canadian Library Association, 1900-1975." In *Livre, bibliothèque et culture québécoise: Mélanges offerts à Edmond Desrochers, s.j.*, ed.Georges-A. Chartrand, 2: 761-99. Montréal: ASTED, 1977.
— "The Canadian Library Position." *Library Review* 84 (winter 1947): 318-20.
— "A Century of Periodical Indexing." *CLAB* 4 (Dec. 1947): 78-81.
— "CLA – ABC and Recruitment Materials." *CLAB* 13 (April 1957): 225-30.
— "Cooperation in Canada." *Library Trends* 24 (Oct. 1975): 399-415.
— *Developing Public Libraries in Canada, 1535-1983: The Alberta Letts Memorial Lecture.* Dalhousie University Libraries and Dalhousie University School of Library Service Occasional Papers Series, No. 9. Halifax, N.S., 1975.
— "The First American Book Festival." *CLAB* 13 (Dec. 1956): 106-7, 109.
— "Libraries." In *Encyclopedia Canadiana*, 6: 132-8.
— "Libraries for Everybody." *CLAB* 10 (June 1954): 250.
— "Libraries in the Life of the Canadian Nation, 1931-1967." MA diss., University of Chicago, 1969. Copy in the Faculty of Information Studies Library, University of Toronto.
— "Library Associations and Education for Librarianship." In *Encyclopedia Canadiana*, 6: 138.
— "Library History of Canada: A Panoramic Survey." *Library History Review* 1 (Dec. 1974): 65-98; 2 (March 1975): 82-106.
— "National Libraries: France." *CLAB* 3 (Dec. 1946): 32-4.
— "National Libraries: Their Organization and Functions." Term paper, University of Chicago, 15 Aug. 1946. Copy in the E.H. Morton file in the Library Development Office, National Library of Canada.
— "Promoting Library Service 1955." *CLAB* 12 (June 1956): 221-4.
— "Raising the Status of Canadian Women." *Queen's Quarterly* 78 (1971): 304-8.
— "Report on Legislative Library." In *Journals of the Legislative Assembly of the*

Province of New Brunswick from the 12th February to the 26th March, 1931, 7-15. Fredericton, 1931.
— "These Years of CLA-ACB, 1955/1960." *CL* 17 (May 1961): 294-395.
— *Trinidad and Tobago: Development of Library Services.* Serial No. 3044/RMO.RD/DBA. Paris: Unesco, 1974.
— "20 Years A-Growing 1944-1964: CLC *Bulletin*, CLA *Bulletin*, *Canadian Library.*" *CL* 20 (May 1964): 291-3.
— "Visiting Some of Canada's Libraries." *CLCB* 2, no. 4 (April 1946): 67-8.
— et al. "Ontario Library Association: The Second Quarter Century 1926-1951." Issued as *OLR* 36 (May 1952): part II.
"Morton, Elizabeth Homer." In *The Canadian Who's Who*, 1973-75.
"Morton, Elizabeth Homer." In *Current Biography Yearbook, 1961*, ed. Charles Moritz, 324-5. New York: H.W. Wilson Co., 1961.
Morton, John. *John Morton of Trinidad ... Journals, Letters and Papers.* Ed. Sarah E. Morton. Toronto: Westminster Co., 1916.
Mount, Graeme S. *Presbyterian Missions to Trinidad and Puerto Rico.* Hantsport, N.S.: Lancelot Press, 1983.
M[owat], A[ngus] "Glory Be! The Canadian Library Association, Association Canadienne des Bibliothèques." *OLR* 30 (Aug. 1946): 227-56.
National Council of Women of Canada. *The Lady Aberdeen Library on the History of Women.* [s.l., 1967].
National Library Act. *Revised Statutes of Canada.* 1952, c. 330.
National Library of Canada. *Research Collections in Canadian Libraries, I. Universities, 1. Prairie Provinces.* Ottawa, 1972.
"Newspaper Microfilming Project / Microfilms de journaux: Catalogue No. 5." *CLAB* 11 (April 1955): 233-50.
"Obituaries ... Morton, Elizabeth Homer." In *The ALA Yearbook: A Review of Library Events 1977*, 210. Chicago: American Library Association, 1978.
The Ontario Library Association: An Historical Sketch, 1900-1925. Toronto: University of Toronto Press, 1926.
Peel, Bruce. "From the President of CLA: CLA Restructuring: Feedback." *Feliciter* 15, no. 1-2 (Sept./Oct. 1969): 1-13.
—, ed. *Librarianship in Canada, 1946 to 1967: Essays in Honour of Elizabeth Homer Morton / Le Bibliothécariat au Canada de 1946 à 1967: Hommages à Elizabeth Homer Morton.* Victoria, B.C.: Printed for the Canadian Library Association by the Morriss Printing Co., 1968.
— "The Microfilm Project of the Canadian Library Association." *Microform Review* 3 (April 1974): 106-7.
Preisman, Sophia. "In Memoriam." *Feliciter* 24, no. 3 (March 1978): 10.
"Proposed Canadian Library Council." *OLR* 25 (Aug. 1941): 228-30.

"Retirements: Elizabeth Homer Morton." *OLR* 52 (June 1968): 92.
Ridington, John. "Canadian Library Association." *ALAB* 24 (1930): 394-5.
Royal Architectural Institute of Canada. *Libraries in Canada Today.* Ottawa: Canadian Library Association [1959]. Reprinted from *RAIC Journal*, April 1959.
— *Library Buildings for Canada.* Ottawa: Canadian Library Association, [1947]; reprinted 1956. Reprinted from *RAIC Journal*, Feb. 1947.
Savides, Danae V. "A History of the Canadian Library Association." BLS term paper, McGill University, 1970. Copy in the Library Development Office, National Library of Canada.
Stuart-Stubbs, Basil. "An Introduction to the Association Canadienne des Bibliothécaires de Langue Française: Its History, Role, and Relationshipto the Canadian Library Association." *Feliciter* 13, no. 9 (May 1969): 3-20.
— "The Librarians of Québec and the Canadian Library Association." In *Livre, bibliothèque et culture québécoise: Mélanges offerts à Edmond Desrochers, s.j.*, ed. Georges-A. Chartrand, 1: 371-84. Montréal: ASTED, 1977.
T[remaine], M[arie]. "Elizabeth H. Morton." *OLR* 28 (Aug. 1944): 314-5.
Talman, James J. "Twenty-two Years of the Microfilm Newspaper Project." *CL* 23 (Sept./Oct. 1968): 140-8.
"Tentative Constitution and By-laws of the Proposed Canadian Library Association." *CLCB* 2, no. 5 (June 1946): 91-4.
"These Years of CLA – ACB, 1960/1966." *CL* 23 (May 1967): 488-521. "Addenda and Corrigenda" published in *CL* 25 (Sept.-Oct. 1968): 149-50.
Thomison, Dennis. *A History of the American Library Association, 1876-1972.* Chicago: American Library Association, 1978.
Thompson, Ruth F. "Canadian Library Week." *CL* 24 (Nov. 1967): 252-3.
"U.S. Denies Work Permit to Briton after Controversial Academic Appointment." *AL* 9 (Oct. 1978): 507-8.
Waldon, Freda F. "The C.L.A. – The First Twenty Years." In *Librarianship in Canada, 1946 to 1967: Essays in Honour of Elizabeth Homer Morton*, ed. Bruce Peel, 22-37. Victoria, B.C.: Printed for the Canadian Library Association by the Morriss Printing Co., 1968.
Welling, Beatrice W. "Canadian Librarians Meet at the American Library Association." *OLR* 10 (Aug. 1925): 11-12.
"Who's Who: Elizabeth Homer Morton ..." *OLR* 27 (May 1943): 142.
Wilson, Marion C. "Elizabeth Homer Morton." *Special Libraries* 68 (Dec. 1977): 466.
Yeo, Ron. "Tribute to Elizabeth Morton." *CLJ* 37 (Oct. 1980): 357.

Index